MiG Killers

USAF F-4 and F-105

MiG Killers

of the Vietnam War

1965-1973

Donald J. McCarthy, Jr.

Schiffer Military History
Atglen, PA

Dedication

For my wife Lynda, daughter Keleen, and her husband Ken
and
my beloved grandchildren, Tyler and Leah

Acknowledgments

It would have been impossible to have completed this project without the help of the many people who gave of their time to help. I wish to offer my thanks to those that have given to this project. Many of whom started out as contacts and became friends. I am especially indebted to: Colonel Al Bache, MSgt. Eric Munsell, Major David Erff, USAFR, Don Logan, Axil Bergeson, Jem Aviation, Tom Brewer, Jeff Kolln, Don Jay, Tom Helbing, Ray Leader, Flightleader, Paul Minert, Norm Taylor, Douglas Slowiak, Mike France, Robert Greby, William Peake, John Coon, Larry Wilson, Red River Fighter Pilots Association, Robert F. Dorr, Lou Drendel, Squadron Signal Publication, Werner Hartman, Ralph Wetterhahn, Tom Hansen, W. J. Latham, Lt. Colonel Mark Hammond, ANG, F-4 Phantom Society, Colonel Jerry Stephan, USAF, (Ret), Ladd Doctor, Colonel J. Crumbliss, USAF, (Ret), Tom Viens, Richard Pendelton, Peter Schinkelshoek, Steve Beebe, Mel Mullins, Jerry Sager, Joe Velten, Peter Schlink, Colonel Ken Kerering, USAF (Ret) James Geer, Joe Seaver, Ray Wood, Charles Stewart, Roger Wilkie, Robert Leavitt, General Al Lenski, USAF, (Ret), Major John Shatz, and USAF (Ret), Colonel Ralph L. Kuster, USAF, (Ret)

I wish to offer a special thanks to the following who opened up their photo collection to me; without them this project would never have been completed: Pat Martin, Ron Picciani, Dave Hansen, Richard Kirebow, Dave McNeil, and Jerry Geer.

To my friend Captain William Gene Eskew, who passed away recently. As always I thank you for your help and friendship. In the words of Colonel Howard Bodenhamer, USAF (Ret), "Gene was one hell of a fighter pilot."

Book Design by Ian Robertson.

Library of Congress Control Number: 2005927092

Printed in China.
ISBN: 0-7643-2256-7

We are interested in hearing from authors with book ideas on related topics.

Published by Schiffer Publishing Ltd.
4880 Lower Valley Road
Atglen, PA 19310
Phone: (610) 593-1777
FAX: (610) 593-2002
E-mail: Info@schifferbooks.com.
Visit our web site at: www.schifferbooks.com
Please write for a free catalog.
This book may be purchased from the publisher.
Please include $3.95 postage.
Try your bookstore first.

In Europe, Schiffer books are distributed by:
Bushwood Books
6 Marksbury Avenue
Kew Gardens
Surrey TW9 4JF
England
Phone: 44 (0) 20 8392-8585
FAX: 44 (0) 20 8392-9876
E-mail: Info@bushwoodbooks.co.uk.
Free postage in the UK. Europe: air mail at cost.
Try your bookstore first.

Contents

Introduction

During the air war in Southeast Asia (1965-1973), Untied States Air Force fighters were credited with destroying 137 MiGs in aerial combat. The two principal American fighters responsible for the vast majority of these MiG kills were the McDonnell Douglas F-4 Phantom II and the Republic F-105 Thunderchief. Of the 137 MiGs destroyed in air-to-air battles, 107 1/2 were shot down by the F-4 Phantom II, while 27 1/2 were credited to the F-105 Thunderchief. The other two enemy MiGs were credited to B-52 tail gunners.

There were 88 individual F-4 Phantoms and 25 individual Thunderchiefs credited with aerial combat victories. Presented in this book is what I believe may be the most complete photo collection of Phantoms and Thunderchiefs credited with aerial victories during the Vietnam era. Of the total 113 individual Phantoms and Thunderchiefs credited with victories, the reader will discover photographs of 106 of these historic aircraft. Among the photographs, the reader will discover, are photographs of the only F-4 Phantom to down six MiGs; the jet flown by Captain Richard "Steve" Ritchie, when on 28 August 1972 he distinguished himself as the first Air Force ACE of the war. Also shown are the three different Phantoms flown by Colonel Robin Olds, Commander of the 8th TFW, crediting him with four MiG kills. Photographs of the first United States Air Force Phantoms to claim MiG kills during the Vietnam War, and last but not least, photographs of the seven United States Air Force F-4Cs credited with downing seven MiG 21s during Operation Bolo are also included.

The reader will further discover photographs of F-105 Thunderchiefs that flew countless combat missions into the skies of North Vietnam, not only dropping their bombs on the most heavily defended targets in the history of aerial warfare, but also fighting many air battles with North Vietnamese MiGs. Photographs are shown of the F-105F flown by Major Leo K. Thorsness when he earned the Medal of Honor. Also depicted are photographs of the only F-105D to claim three MiGs during the war. Many of the photographs are wartime photographs that show the weapon systems of the period: Sidewinder and Sparrow missiles; MK-82 500-pound bombs; cluster weapons; Shrike missiles, etc. Many post war photographs of these historic aircraft are during service with Air National Guard and Air Force Reserve Units.

Accompanying each of the photographs is detailed information in regard to the aircrews, units, call signs of the individual aircraft, primary weapon systems used in the destruction of the enemy aircraft, and narratives regarding each air battle. The information used in these narratives was compiled from the Air Force publication "Aces & Aerial Victories," by the Office of Air Force History, Maxwell Air Force Base, Alabama, and from the original MiG claim statements filed by the aircrews. The information is quoted directly, or paraphrased from these sources for the purpose of historical accuracy.

Also pictured in this book is the North American F-100D flown by Captain Donald W. Kilgus on 4 April 1965, when he claimed an enemy MiG 17. This particular F-100D may have, in fact, obtained the first MiG kill of the air war in Vietnam.

I have included in this project, with the kind permission of the authors, two accounts of MiG engagements that took place during the Vietnam era. The first involves the MiG kill of 1st Lt. Karl W. Richter on 21 September 1966. In an article written by Ralph Wetterhahn that appeared in the November 2000 issue of *Air & Space*, he offers a look at the air battle from the North Vietnamese pilots' point of view. I have also included, with the permission of Lou Drendel and Squadron/Signal Publication, the MiG engagement of 1st Lt. Dave B. Waldrop III on 23 August 1967. This account gives the reader an excellent perspective of air combat from the cockpit. Also included is the verbatim account of Colonel Robin Olds' MiG kill on 2 January 1967, during Operation Bolo. This account was taken directly from his original MiG claim statement.

During the research of this project there were a number of source documents used to identify the individual F-4s and F-105s credited with aerial combat victories. The primary document used is what I refer to as the Brewer List. The Brewer List is a list of F-4C, D, and E model Phantoms, along with F-105s that has been compiled by Tom Brewer of the Air Force Museum, Dayton, Ohio, along with other historians. Tom Brewer and others discovered that, as incredible as it may sound, the Air Force did not keep a record of the serial numbers of aircraft that shot down MiGs in Southeast Asia. He and others have searched for many years to come up with the Brewer List as it appears today. The list identifies by tail number the aircraft credited with a MiG kill, as well as the aircrews.

The Brewer List does have a number of holes or uncertainties regarding some of the tail numbers, particularly as it relates to the MiG kills of the 555th Tactical Fighter Squadron in April 1966.

The list identifies three F-4Cs as being the jets flown during April 1966 MiG engagements. The daily operational records of the 8th TFW, 555th TFS, confirms these F-4Cs as in fact being the correct Phantoms flown during those MiG Kill missions. However, there is evidence to suggest that these Phantoms were not assigned with the 555th TFS during April 1966. In any event, in the absence of any other known tail numbers I have included photographs of 64-689, 64-696, and 64-697 in this project in case the records of the 8th Tactical Fighter Wing may be correct.

To this very day, there are two F-4Cs and four F-105Ds whose tail numbers remain unknown. The tail number of a fifth F-105D has for many years been surrounded with uncertainty. The fifth Thud I refer to is that flown by 1st Lt. Karl Richter during his MiG kill of 21 September 1966. In regard to the four unknown F-105s, two may now be accounted for.

In researching this project, I was very fortunate to come in contact with Major John Shatz, USAF (Ret), who in 1966 was a Captain in the United States Air Force. Major Shatz was at the time a maintenance officer with the 421st Tactical Fight Squadron of the 388th Tactical Fighter Wing at Korat RTAFB. During my contact with Major Shatz, he told me that he was very familiar with the certain historical events that took place at Korta RTAFB during 1966, and in fact, has many of these events documented in his personal records.

Regarding the 18 August 1966 MiG kill of Major Kenneth T. Blank, the following notation was discovered in Major Shatz's historical notes that indicates the tail number of the F-105D flown by Major Blank was in fact 60-458. The notation reads; "Blank-#2-34-17-458 18/08 expended (680?)." The simple translation of the notation is:

"Ken Blank — Honda 02 - 34th TFS - MiG 17 - tail number 60-458 - August 18-expended (680?) rounds of 20-mm."

All of which fits Major Blank. He was in fact call sign Honda 02, flying with the 34th Tactical Fighter Squadron, and destroyed a MiG 17, with 458 being the tail number of the aircraft he flew, and 18/08 being August 18 the date of his kill.

As mentioned, there has always been a degree of uncertainty surrounding the aircraft flown by 1st Lt. Karl Richter during his MiG kill mission. However, there is no uncertainty in the mind of Major Shatz. His notes and personal recollection identify F-105D, tail number 59-1766 as being the aircraft.*

"Karl was flying 59-1766 when he scored his MiG 17 kill. It became his assigned 'Bird' that day. I recall talking with Lt. Colonel Fred Tracy, who at the time was the 421st TFS Squadron Commander, about painting Karl's name on the aircraft. We also decided that a 5" red star with the type aircraft killed, date, and ordinance expenditure would also be placed on the aircraft."

Coincidently, F-105D tail number 59-1766 was also the aircraft flown by 1st Lt. Karl Richter on his 100th mission into North Vietnam.

Information regarding another previously unknown F-105, flown by Major Fredrick G. Tolman on 19 April 1967, is also covered within this book.

The violent air battles in the skies of Hanoi, Haiphong, Phuc Yen, Kep airfield, and countless other places in Vietnam have long since passed into history. The legendary F-4 Phantom and F-105 Thunderchiefs have long since flown their last combat missions, and now rest in Air Museums, on grassy knolls, and high on pedestals in recognition of the many Air Force pilots who every day flew these old war horses into harms way.

Donald J. McCarthy, Jr.
Detective Commander (Ret)
Waterford Police Department
Waterford, Connecticut
2005

*It should also be noted that part of the many duties of Major Shatz during his tour at Korat RTAFB was to design the MiG kill markings to be used to identify aircraft of the 421st TFS credited with a MiG kill, and to ensure that the aircraft were so marked.

F-100D / 55-2894

2nd AD / 416th TFS

Capt. Donald W. Kilgus

Pictured below is F-100D, tail number 55-2895, of the 416th Tactical Fighter Squadron, Da Nang Air Base, Vietnam. Captain Don Kilgus flew this particular F-100D on 4 April 1965, when he engaged a North Vietnamese MiG 17 in aerial combat. The outcome of this air battle has been the subject of much debate by historians over the years. However, in the mind of Captain Don Kilgus and many others, there is no debate. The MiG was "destroyed" as a direct result of the air battle. In spite of the ongoing debate, Captain Don Kilgus was credited with only a probable victory by the United States Air Force.

Information has come to light since the end of the Vietnam War, and the establishment of diplomatic relations with the Peoples Republic of Vietnam, which I suspect was never considered in the Kilgus claim. Although the Vietnamese still remain tight lipped over events of the war, they have admitted to the loss of three MiGs during air battles on 4 April 1965. Not only do they admit to the loss of three MiG 17s, they go as far as to identify the pilots by name and their unit. The three Vietnamese pilots have been identified as Pham Giay, Le Minh Huan, and Tran Nguyen Nam, all of the 921st Fighter Regiment. The sole North Vietnamese pilot to survive the air battle of 4 April 1965, Lt. Tran Hanh, reported that the three MiGs lost on 4 April 1965 were lost to American fighters (*MiG 17 and MiG 19 Units of the Vietnam War*; Istvan Toperczer; Osprey Combat Books).

In the '60s the United States Air Force conducted a study of air-to-air encounters in Southeast Asia. This project code name was Red Baron. The MiG engagement of Captain Don Kilgus is included within the Red Baron report and identified as Event III-2. A very interesting notation appears in Event III-2 from the Red Baron Report:

"Other sources list a probably MiG 17 kill due to 20-mm cannon fire at this time and date and is most likely the result of this encounter."

Another thing that struck the author about the Red Baron Report was the combat narrative, wherein the dynamics of the air battle are described by Captain Don Kilgus. The dynamics of the air battle suggested to the author—a non-pilot—that the MiG could not have survived the engagement as described.

In 2003 I requested a good friend to review Event III-2 of the Red Baron Report. Unlike myself, my friend is a combat pilot. Former Air Force Captain Gene Eskew was an F-105 pilot who flew over 100 combat missions into North Vietnam. On 19 April 1967 Captain Eskew was credited with engaging in air combat a number of MiG 17s. As a result of the air battle he was credited by the Air Force with destroying one MiG 17, and probably a second MiG 17.

Captain Eskew told me as a result of reviewing the Red Baron report:

"In my mind there's no question that Captain Don Kilgus shot down the MiG 17. Captain Don Kilgus said he saw puffs and sparks on the vertical tail of the MiG after he fired. He Got a Kill! There's no way a MiG 17 can continue flying after being hammered by 20-mm cannon fire. I can't remember the rate-of-fire of the F-100 cannon. However, even a couple of 20-mm hits would damage a MiG so badly it couldn't fly, let alone recover from the dive described in the Red Baron Report.

Also Captain Kilgus' description of the engagement is absolutely believable. He describes firing two short bursts at the MiG, then one long burst. He fired a total of 300-400 rounds, according to the Red Baron report. That's consistent with a MiG engagement by an experienced pilot.

There were several rules of a hassle with MiGs. For example, fly the aircraft into the proper position, then fire. Always shoot first. Don't keep shooting if you're not hitting your target. Fly the aircraft into a better position, then shoot again. Don't get tunnel vision on your target. Tunnel vision on one MiG will allow another MiG to get into firing position on you. Don't get too concerned

with eyeballing to see if a MiG you hit went down. Someone else will confirm your kill. Break away and look for someone else to fight.

During his engagement with the MiG 17, Captain Don Kilgus followed all of these rules, and there is no doubt in my mind (Captain Gene Eskew) he got the first MiG kill of the Vietnam War."

In 2003 I contacted Mrs. Kay Kilgus, wife of retired Air Force Colonel Don Kilgus, in an attempt to locate any documents the late Colonel may have had in regard to his MiG encounter in April 1965. Mrs. Kilgus informed me that any documents that did exist regarding the events have long since been lost or misplaced as a result of her and the Colonels' many military moves. However, Mrs, Kilgus did relate to me an incident that took place while she and the Colonel were stationed at Luke Air Force Base, Arizona. Mrs. Kilgus went on to tell me that Colonel Kilgus had been contacted (*telephone call*) by a Major Custer in regard to the Colonels' MiG kill claim. Although she can't recall all the facts and circumstances of the Colonels' phone call with Major Custer, she does recall that her husband told her that the telephone call was in regard to his MiG engagement during the War. Mrs. Kilgus went on to tell me she also recalls there was a conversation regarding compromising a source in the North. Mrs. Kilgus made available to me three United States Air Force message numbers from the Vietnam era that she identified as having been provided to Colonel Kilgus by Major Custer.

After talking with Mrs. Kilgus a few questions came to mind. Who is Major Custer? Why does Major Custer go out of his way to contact Colonel Kilgus? What is the source in the North?

My guess was that Major Custer was directly involved with the Air Force "Red Baron Report," also felt that Colonel Kilgus downed his MiG in April '65, and felt that Colonel Kilgus should resubmit his claim

After locating a copy of the Red Baron Report, there in black and white, in the foreword of the document, Major Ralph L. Kuster, Jr.—he was indeed involved with the Red Baron Report.

After this discovery I knew instantly who he was. Major Ralph L. Kuster took what can only be described as the single most famous aerial photograph of the Vietnam Air War. The photograph has appeared on the covers of books, in articles and books related to air-to-air combat, and you can't see a documentary on the Air War without seeing this photograph. The photograph is from the gun camera of Major Ralph L. Kuster's F-105, and depicts the death of a North Vietnamese MiG 17 he shot down on 3 June 1967. Flying as Hambone 02 he engaged a MiG 17 with his 20-mm cannon, causing the MiG's left wing to explode.

With very little effort I was able to locate Major Ralph L. Kuster, Jr., now a retired United States Air Force Colonel. I have exchanged in dialogue with Colonel Kuster over the Kilgus matter, as well as other issues. In regards to Colonel Kilgus' MiG engagement of April 1965, the following is the account of Colonel Kuster's recollections of the matter:

"This statement concerns a series of occurrences which happened some thirty-seven years ago, but which I believe I recall very well. The following considers verification of a MiG 17 'kill' by Don Kilgus while flying a F-100 over North Vietnam.

First, some background. After completing my 100 mission F-105 tour of duty in South East Asia (SEA) flying out of Korat RTAFB I was assigned to the Weapon System Evaluation Group (WESG), with offices across the street from the Pentagon. My position was one of four extra analysts assigned temporarily, because a particular analysis required firsthand knowledge of combat in South East Asia. The study team was the first Red Baron Analysis, 'The Study of Air-to-Air Combat in SEA.' The analysis was conducted using information collated from MiG encounters reported to us via tape. A different team had previously taped air crew interviews at the air crew's station. We produced the first four Volumes before turning the Study over to Nellis AFB for follow-on analysis. Don Kilgus was one of those pilots interviewed by the team.

In 1968, while converting those air-to-air encounters from verbal taped conversation into black and white script and diagrams, the F-100 encounters were assigned to my desk, along with other categories. At that time there were no MiG Kills attributed to F-100 aircraft. On a search through other classified sources that routinely matched up with verbal reports, I happened to note a reported MiG 17 crash in North Vietnam (NVN) on a particular day and time which cross-checked with the verbal report of Don Kilgus and other pilots of his flight.

In order to clarify the issue of a match, I talked with Don Kilgus after locating his current assignment, and discussed the encounter with him on the telephone. His recollection was good, in that he thought he hit the MiG, but was not positive of damage because of limited visibility due to haze at the low altitude and the high speed of the aircraft involved. The other classified source identified the MiG 17 as being damaged, but able to fly some distance before crashing. I advised him that I thought the MiG that crashed was most probably damaged by his fire, and he should pursue the assignment of that MiG Kill to him, and that I would help when possible. However, I could not discuss too many details over the phone because of the classified nature of the information.

Unfortunately, I was never again contacted regarding the occurrence until recently." - Ralph L. Kuster, Jr., Colonel, USAF (Ret).

According to Mrs. Kilgus, sometime later, while her husband was at the Air War College, he tried to locate the three Air Force messages mentioned in the original phone call from Colonel Kuster. He, too, found the official files difficult to work through, and never located the documents. I can relate to this, as I have also attempted to locate the elusive Vietnam era messages with no luck. The search continues.

With the admission of the Peoples Republic of Vietnam to the loss of three MiG 17s on 4 April 1965, the account of the air battle described in the Air Force study known as the Red Baron Report, along with the information provided by Colonel Ralph L. Kuster, there can be little doubt that Captain Kilgus downed the first MiG of the Vietnam War.

The in-flight photograph of F-100D, tail number 55-2894, was taken during the air war in Southeast Asia while she was assigned to the 416th TFS. The second photograph, provided by Robert F. Dorr, depicts Captain Kilgus in the cockpit of an F-105F. Dave Hansen provided the third photograph in this series. This unique and rare photograph depicts the canopy area of Captains Don Kilgus' and Ted Lowry's F-105F. Clearly visible on the canopy rail, in front of Captain Kilgus' name, is a red star denoting his MiG kill of 4 April 1965. According to Colonel Lowry, USAF (Ret), the reason for the red star on their Thud was because there was absolutely no doubt in Captain Kilgus' mind that he destroyed the MiG.

Colonel Ted Lowry highly respected Colonel Kilgus' abilities as a fighter pilot, and has been quoted as saying, "He would have been great on Rickenbacker's wing."

MiG Killers
F-4C, D, & E

F-4C / 63-7489
35th TFW / 480th TFS

Capt. William J. Swendner
1st Lt. Duane A. Buttell, Jr.
Unknown 01

F-4C -18-MC 63-7489 - Credited with downing a MiG 21 on 14 July 1966 while providing MiG cover for an Iron Hand flight of three F-105s, Capt. Swendner and Lt. Buttell fired three Sidewinder missiles at the MiG. The third missile went up the MiG's tailpipe and blew the MiG into pieces. In this 1966-1967 era photograph taken at Da Nang Air Base, tail number 63-7489 is uniquely marked with a large silhouette of a MiG 21 on the nose of the aircraft. On 27 December 1967, F-4C 63-7489 was lost in combat to automatic weapons fire while on a mission over North Vietnam. (T. Hansen via D. Hansen)

F-4C / 63-7535
366th TFW / 480th TFS

1st Lt. Wilbur J. Latham, Jr.
1st Lt. Klaus J. Klaus
Opal 02

F-4C-19-MC 63-7535 - On 5 November 1966, Opal flight was tasked to provide MIGCAP for an EB-66 that was operating deep within North Vietnamese airspace. During the mission the EB-66 was attacked by two MiG 21s. The lead MiG fired an air-to-air missile at the EB-66 but missed. In the ensuing air battle Opal lead and Opal 02 downed both of the MiGs with air-to-air missiles:

"Latham saw a MiG pull up in front of him and his back seater, Lt. Klause, and he launched a Sidewinder. The missile exploded near the MiG's tail pipe and the pilot ejected."

F-4C 63-7535 was lost during a rocket attack at Da Nang Air Base on 15 July 1967. This aircraft was one of five F-4Cs assigned to the 390th TFS that were heavily damaged or destroyed during the attack. The series of photographs presented hear depict the aftermath of the rocket attack. The first photograph was obtained from Jerry Sanger, who at the time was assigned to the 366th SP Squadron. It depicts one of the damaged F-4Cs and the wreckage of another Phantom. The second and third photos were provided by Mel Mullins of the 366th MMS Squadron, and again depict the aftermath and clean up of the attack of 15 July 1967. The second photograph depicts the clean up operation after the attack, and further depicts a second damaged Phantom, as well as a destroyed F-4C being removed. The third photo depicts one of the Air Force's Type 0-11A fire trucks that was also destroyed during the attack. The fire fighters were attempting to put out the fire on one of the burning bomb-loaded F-4s when one or more of the 500-pound bombs detonated, killing all five of the fire fighters. Presently on display at Hollman AFB, NM, is an F-4C that has been remade to represent the 5 November 1965 MiG 21 shoot down of 1st Lts. Latham and Klause. Latham and Klause were flying as Opal 2 when they downed their MiG while escorting an EB-66 in North Vietnam, near Hanoi. (J. Sanger / M. Mullins / M. Hammond via Latham)

HO
535

F-4C / 63-7541
366th TFW / 480th TFS

Maj. James E. Tuck
1st Lt. John J. Rabeni, Jr.
Opal 01

F-4C-19-MC 63-7541 - On November 5, 1966, in the northeast section of North Vietnam, near Hanoi, Maj. Tuck and 1st. Lt. Rabeni, flying as Opal lead, engaged and destroyed a MiG 21. Opal lead downed the MiG by employing the AIM-7 Sparrow missile. The crew of Opal lead downed one of two MiGs that was attacking an EB-66 near Hanoi and Haiphong. Many years after the air battle, F-4C 63-7541 was still serving with the 136th FIS, New York ANG. The red star outlined in yellow is still on the intake ramp of the aircraft.. (P. Martin Collection)

F-4C / 63-7577
366th TFW / 390th TFS

Maj. Robert G. Dilger
1st Lt. Mack Thies
Stinger 01

F-4C-19-MC 63-7577 - This photograph of 63-7577 was taken at Robins AFB, GA, in November 1964 at a fire power demonstration. On 1 May 1967, while assigned to the 366th TFW / 390th TFS, she was credited with downing a MiG 17. At the time of the engagement, Stinger lead was part of a MIGCAP barrier flight. Stinger lead's Maj. Dilger and Lt. Thies detected two or three enemy aircraft approaching from their 12 o'clock position. During the ensuing air battle Stinger lead fired a number of AIM-7 and AIM-9 missiles at one of the MiGs, but failed to hit the mark. On the fourth pass the MiG being pursued broke hard right and struck the ground while attempting to avoid a missile. Ironically, all four members of the 45th TFS, as seen in the photograph, were later credited with the United States Air Force's first two aerial victories of the Vietnam War on 10 July '65: Captains Kenneth E. Holcombe (2nd from the left); Ronald C. Anderson (6th from the left); Thomas Roberts (1st from the right); and Arthur C. Clark (2nd from the right). On 26 June 1967, F-4C 63-7577 was lost to a MiG of the Peoples Republic of China Air Force. The air-to-air combat took place in the area of Hainan Island. (D. Whitney via L. Wilson)

F-4C / 63-7589
8th TFW / 555th TFS

1st Lt. Ralph F. Wetterhahn
1st Lt. Jerry K. Sharp
Olds 02

F-4C-19-MC 63-7589 - On 2 January '67, 1st Lts. Ralph F. Wetterhahn and Jerry K. Sharp from the 555th TFS downed a MiG 21 with an AIM-7 missile during "Operation Bolo." Olds 02 launched two Sparrow missiles at a MiG 21. The missile impacted the MiG just forward of the stabilizer. The MiG was observed to be shredding large portions of the aft section as it went into a flat spin. Loaded here with both missiles and bombs, tail number 63-7589 is ready for another mission into North Vietnam. This photograph was taken sometime during 1967 while assigned to the 497th TFS at Ubon RTAFB. (R. Picciani Collection)

F-4C / 63-7623
8th TFW / 433rd TFS

Maj. John R. Pardo
1st Lt. Stephen A. Wayne
Tampa 03

F-4C-20-MC 63-7623 - On 20 May 1967 Tampa 03, crewed by Maj. Pardon and Lt. Wayne of the 8th TFW operating out of Ubon, RTAFB, were flying MIGCAP for a strike force of F-105s. Tampa flight engaged an enemy force of between 12 to 14 MiG 17s. Four of the MiGs were destroyed in less than 10 minutes. Pardo and Wayne downed the fourth MiG of the encounter with a Sidewinder air-to-air missile. F-4C 63-7623 is depicted in this post Vietnam photograph with the markings of the 113th TFS of the Indiana ANG out of Terre Haute. Located on the splitter plate is the red star denoting the 20 May 1967 MiG kill. (P. Martin Collection)

F-4C / 63-7647
8th TFW / 555th TFS

Capt. Richard M. Pascoe
Capt. Norman E. Wells
Chicago 02

F-4C-20-MC 63-7647 - On 5 June 1967, Captains Pascoe and Wells downed their second MiG of the Vietnam War. During this mission they were flying in the number two position of Chicago flight, on the wing of Col. Robin Olds, when the air-to-air encounter took place. The MiG they engaged was totally destroyed after being hit by two Sidewinder missiles fired by Chicago 02. In this photograph, while serving with the Oregon Air National Guards, 123rd FIS, 142nd FIG, 63-7647 is clearly marked with two MiG kills. Only one can be officially accounted for at this time. (P. Martin Collection)

F-4C / 63-7650
8th TFW / 555th TFS

1st Lt. Jerry W. Jameson
1st Lt. Douglas B. Rose
Unknown 04

F-4C-20-MC 63-7650 - Seen wearing the wraparound camouflage of the Vietnam era while serving with the 170th TFS, 183rd TFG of the Illinois ANG, this particular F-4C and its aircrew, Lts. Jameson and Rose, were previously credited with downing a MiG 21 with an AIM-9 missile on 16 September 1966, while assigned to the 555th TFS. The air battle took place over North Vietnam in the area of the Dap Cau Railroad and Highway Bridge. In the second photograph, 63-7650 is unceremoniously displayed at Davis Monthan AFB, after having been cannibalized for parts. (R. Picciani Collection/D. Erff)

F-4C / 63-7652
8th TFW / 433rd TFS

1st Lt. Lawrence J. Glynn, Jr.
1st Lt. Lawrence E. Cary
Rambler 02
"No Photo Available"

F-4C-20-MC 63-7652 - On 2 January 1967, Lts. Glynn and Cary were credited with the seventh and final aerial victory of "Operation Bolo." During the action Glynn and Cary fired two Sparrow missiles, one of which guided to the MiG and destroyed it. On 9 May 1967 this Phantom was written off as a non combat loss after the left main tire failed on take off.

F-4C / 63-7668
8th TFW / 555th TFS

Col. Robin Olds
1st Lt. William D. Lafever
Flamingo 01

F-4C-21-MC 63-7668 - This F-4C was flown by Col. Robin Olds and Lt. Lefever on 4 May 1967 when they engaged and downed a MiG 21 with an AIM-9 missile while on a MIGCAP mission over North Vietnam. In this photograph the splitter plate of 63-7668 is clearly marked with a red star trimmed in yellow, identifying her MiG kill of 4 May 1967. On 27 January 1968 F-4C 63-7688 was operating with the 366th TFW, 390th TFS when lost to 37mm anti-aircraft artillery fire. (R. Picciani Collection)

F-4C / 63-7680
8th TFW / 555th TFS
8th TFW / 433rd TFS

Col. Robin Olds
1st Lt. Charles C. Clifton
Olds 01

Lt. Col. Fred A. Haeffner
1st Lt. Michael R. Bever
Harpoon 03

F-4C-21-MC 63-7680 - On 2 January 1967, aircraft of the 8th Tactical Fighter Wing, under the command of Colonel Robin Olds, engaged in "Operation Bolo." Operation Bolo was a specially designed mission to lure North Vietnamese MiGs into air-to-air combat. As a direct result of air battles on 2 January 1967, a total of seven North Vietnamese MiG 21s were downed. The following account of Colonel Robin Olds' MiG kill is taken directly from his MiG claim statement. The statement was obtained as a result of a Freedom of Information request from the records collection of the National Archives:

"I Colonel Robin Olds, Commander 8th Tactical Fighter Wing, make the following statement in substantiation of my claim for the destruction in air combat of one MiG 21 aircraft over North Vietnam on 2 January 1967.

On that day I was serving as mission commander for a force of F-4C, F-104, and F-105 aircraft performing a planned fighter sweep in the Hanoi area. Fourteen flights of F-4's, six flights of F-105 Iron Hand, and four flights of F-104's participated in the sweep, supported in normal fashion by B-66 ECM, RC-121 Big Eye, and KC-135 Tankers. The B-66's were provided escort by additional F-4C aircraft.

As mission commander I flew lead position in Olds flight, first in the stream of F-4C's planned to converge on Phuc Yen airfield. Time on target (TOT) was 1400G, and was made good. No definite radar contacts were made as we ingressed on a heading of 145-

degrees. Weather at the time was solid undercast, tops estimated 7000 feet, ceiling unknown. I led Olds flight past Phuc Yen for approximately 14 to 18 NM, then turned so as to cross Phuc Yen on a reciprocal heading. As the turn was completed Olds 3 picked up a radar contact low at 12 o'clock, high closure rate. He gained a lock on and was instructed to attack. Steering dot information put the flight into a 10 to 15-degree dive.

Just as we neared the top of the undercast, radar lock broke. The target was under or in the overcast and had passed beneath us on an opposite heading.

I led the flight on past the airfield once again, called the ingressing F-4 flights, Ford and Rambler that missiles free was no longer in effect and turned my flight back southeast. Just as we again crossed Phuc Yen, Ford flight arrived on time. Everything then happened at once. Ford called a MiG 21 closing on Olds flight at their 7 o'clock. Olds 2 saw the MiG simultaneously. Additional MiGs were popping up through the clouds. Olds lead initiated a left turn of sufficient intensity to throw off the attacking MiGs aim, but without breaking Olds flight integrity. A defensive split by elements was automatically taken.

After 90-degrees of turn in this modified break. I sighted an aircraft at my 11 o'clock in a left turn, slightly low, about a miles and a quarter away. I closed on this target for positive identification, not having seen a MiG before and by now uncertain of the exact location of all members of Ford flight. The target was positively identified as a MiG 21, silver in color, too distant for markings to be seen. I instructed the pilot to go bore sight, put the pipper on the target, and called for lock-on a full system operation. I was setting us up for an AIM-7 attack. Closure was enough to necessitate haste in establishing the proper attack parameter. We achieved a lock-on, went full system, I centered the steering dot (interlocks 'in') and pressed-released, pressed and held the trigger. Two AIM-7's launched and appeared to track. At that moment we lost radar lock on, having passed beyond minimum range, and the missiles had no chance to guide. I quickly selected HEAT, put the pipper on the MiG as he was disappearing into the overcast, received an indistinct missile growl and fired one AIM-9, knowing the missile had little chance to guide.

During the first encounter, Olds 2 was busily engaged in pursuing the original MiG 21 that had closed behind my flight. In addition, as I closed on the MiG that evaded in the cloud deck, I had another in sight at my 10 o'clock, in a left turn, and just above the clouds. I then turned my attention to the second MiG. I pulled sharp left, turned inside him, pulled my nose up about 30-degrees above the horizon, rechecked my missile switches and ready panel, switched fuel to internal wing transfer, barrel rolled to the right, held my position upside down above and behind the MiG until the proper angular deflection and range parameters were satisfied, completed the rolling maneuver, and fell in behind and below the MiG 21 at his 7 o'clock position at about .95 mach. Range was 4500 feet, angle off 15-degrees. The MiG 21 obligingly pulled up well above the horizon and exactly down sun. I put the pipper on his tail pipe, received a perfect growl, squeezed the trigger once, hesitated, then once again. The first Sidewinder leapt in front and within a split second, turned left in a definite and beautiful collision course correction. I did not take my eyes off the first Sidewinder and consequently did not see precisely what the second missile did. It appeared to my peripheral vision to have guide also. The first missile went slightly down, then arced gracefully up, heading for impact. Suddenly the MiG 21 erupted in a brilliant flash of orange flame. A complete wing separated and flew back in the air stream, together with a mass of smaller debris. The MiG swapped ends immediately, and tumbled forward for an instant. It then fell, twisted, corkscrewing, tumbling, lazily toward the top of the clouds. No pilot ejection occurred above the overcast. The MiG continued to fall and disappeared into the clouds. The form of the aircraft was clearly visible during many separate instants. It was minus one wing and the other presented the wedge shape, sharply swept leading edge, straight trailing edge, characteristic of the MiG 21.

I continued my left turn, looked for other MiGs, checked my fuel gage, and gave the order to egress, knowing Olds 4, was not obtaining fuel from his centerline tank, and was at bingo fuel.

We left the battle area as Ford flight broke off its engagement and Rambler flight became engaged. We proceeded to home station as briefed."

The second MiG kill for this fighter was recorded on 13 May 1967, when Lt. Col. Haeffner and Lt. Bever, flying as Harpoon 03, destroyed a MiG 17 with the AIM-7 air-to-air missile. F-4C 63-7680 appears in this powerful Frank MacSorley color photograph taken on the ramp at Ubon RTAFB, and is armed with a full complement of Sparrow and Sidewinder missiles. Clearly visible on the splitter plate are two red stars trimmed in yellow, denoting her two kills. The tail section of MiG killer 63-7668 appears in the background. On 20 November 1967, F-4C 63 7680 was lost in combat to automatic weapons fire. (R. Picciani Collection)

F-4C / 63-7683
8th TFW / 555th TFS

Capt. Walter S. Radecker, III
1st Lt. James E. Murray, III
Olds 04

F-4C-21-MC 63-7683 - Photographed on the flight line at Ubon RTAFB in 1967, F-4C 63-7683 was assigned to the 497th TFS. On 2 January 1967 Capt. Radecker and Lt. Murray were flying as Olds 04 in Olds flight when they engaged, fired on, and destroyed the second MiG claimed during "Operation Bolo." This Phantom went on to survive the war, serving last with the Oregon ANG, and was photographed during 1988, still proudly displaying the red star on the splitter plate. (P. Martin Collection/Author)

F-4C / 63-7699
366th TFW / 480th TFS

Maj. Samuel O. Bakke
Capt. Robert W. Lambert
Elgin 01

F-4C-21-MC 63-7699 - On 14 May 1967 Maj. Bakke and Capt. Lambert were flying the lead aircraft in Elgin flight when they downed a MiG 17 with an AIM-7 missile. The AIM-7 missile locked on the MiG, causing an explosion and fire in the right wing root. F-4C tail number 63-7699 was assigned to the 123rd Fighter Interceptor Squadron, Oregon Air National Guard, based at Portland IAP, Oregon, when this photograph was taken. Photographed at Tyndall AFB, FL, on 23 October 1984, during William Tell competition, by Norm Taylor. (N. Taylor Collection)

F-4C / 63-7704
366th TFW / 480th TFS

Capt. James T. Craig, Jr.
1st Lt. James T. Talley
Speedo 03

F-4C-21-MC 63-7704 - This F-4C Phantom recorded its MiG kill on 14 May 1967, when Capt. Craig and Lt. Talley downed a MiG 17 with 20-mm cannon fire after missing the MiG with two Sparrow missiles. Still marked as a MiG killer, F-4C 63-7704 is depicted in this photograph taxiing for another training mission. At the time of this photograph, 63-7704 was operating with the 122nd TFS, 159th TFG, based in New Orleans. The second photograph depicts 63-7704 after being prepared for storage at Davis Monthan AFB. (P. Martin Collection / D. Erff)

F-4C / 63-7710
8th TFW / 555th TFS

Capt. Everett T. Raspberry, Jr.
1st Lt. Robert W. Western
Ford 02

F-4C-21-MC 63-7710 - In this striking in flight photograph, 63-7710 is flying off the wing of another Phantom enroute back to Ubon RTAFB with empty bomb racks after a previous mission into North Vietnam. On 2 January 1967 Capt. Raspberry and Lt. Western were credited with the fourth aerial victory during "Operation Bolo." Raspberry and Western downed their MiG 21 with an AIM-9 Sidewinder air-to-air missile. This F-4C was later lost on 12 June '67, due to a hydraulic systems malfunction. (F. MacSorley via R. Picciani Collection)

F-4C / 64-0660
35th TFW / 390th TFS
366th TFW / 480th TFS

Maj. Wilbur R. Dudley
1st. Lt. Imants Kringelis
Jupiter 03

Maj. James A. Hargrove, Jr.
1st Lt. Stephen H. De Muth
Speedo 01

Maj. Durwood K. Priester
Capt. John E. Pankhurst
Oakland 01

F-4C-21-MC 64-0660 - This F-4C is credited with engaging and destroying three MiG 17s during her war time service. On 12 May 1967 Maj. Dudley and Lt. Kringelis downed the first MiG with an AIM-9 Sidewinder missile while it was in the process of attacking an Air Force EB-66. The second MiG was claimed and credited to Maj. Hargrove and Lt. De Muth on 14 May 1967. Flying as Speedo lead, they downed a MiG 17 with 20-mm cannon fire. Maj. Priester and Capt. Pankhurst were assigned to a MIGCAP flight for an Iron Hand mission in the vicinity of "THUD RIDGE" when they downed the third MiG 17 with 20-mm cannon fire. F-4C 64-0660 was assigned to the 35th Tactical Fighter Squadron, 347th Tactical Fighter Wing, based at Yokota Air Base, Japan, when this photograph was taken in 1968. The first photograph depicts 64-0660 many years after the war, still serving with the New York Air National Guard. The three red stars are still proudly displayed on the aircraft's splitter plate. (P. Martin Collection / C. Stewart via F-4 Phantom Society)

F-4C / 64-673
8th TFW / 433rd TFS

Maj. Philip P. Combies
1st Lt. Daniel L. Lafferty
Ballot 01

F-4C-22-MC 64-0673 - In this May 1968 photograph 64-0673 is in the markings of the 347th Tactical Fighter Wing, based at Yokota Air Base, Japan. On 20 May 1967 Maj. Combies and Lt. Lafferty were flying as Ballot lead during a MIGCAP mission in the area of the Bac Le Railroad Yards in North Vietnam when they engaged a MiG 17. During the air battle, Ballot lead was able to get behind the MiG and fired an AIM-9 with good tone. The missile impacted in the aft fuselage of the MIG, sending it into an uncontrollable dive and hurling it into the ground. The second photograph of 64-0673 is as she appears today after being restored by the Pima Air Museum in Tucson, AZ. (N. Taylor Collection / J. Kolln)

F-4C / 64-679
2nd AD / 45th TFS

Capt. Thomas S. Roberts
Capt. Arthur C. Clark

Mink 04

F-4C-22-MC 64-679 - On 10 July 1965, two F-4 aircrews of the 45th TFS, flying from Ubon Royal Thai Air Base, were officially credited with the first two United States Air Force MiG kills of the Vietnam War. It is not entirely clear as to which aircrew downed the first MiG, as both MiGs were downed within seconds of each other. Capts. Roberts and Clark were flying as part of Mink flight when they fired on and destroyed one of the MiG 17s with one of their AIM-9 missiles. In this black and white air refueling photograph of 64-679, she is heading North with a full complement of Sidewinder and Sparrow missiles on another MIGCAP mission. The second black and white photograph depicts 64-679 years later, still in the SEA camouflage scheme while serving with the Illinois Air National Guard. In this color photograph, 64-679 presents herself as she appears today on display at Misawa Air Base, Japan. (L. Wilson / J. Geer)

ILLINOIS
AF
64 679

U.S. AIR FORCE

F-4C / 64-689
8th TFW / 555th TFS

Capt. Max F. Cameron
1st Lt. Robert E. Evans
Unknown 03

F-4C-22-MC 64-689 - In this Larry Wilson photograph, 64-0689 is part of a flight of F-4Cs engaged in mid-air refueling before heading into North Vietnamese airspace. This photograph depicts the F-4s in the pre-War gull gray over white color scheme. On 23 April 1966, Capt. Cameron and Lt. Evans downed a MiG 17 with an AIM-9 missile. The victory came while part of a MiG Screen flight for a flight of F-105s in the area of the Bac Giang highway and Railroad Bridge, northeast of Hanoi. On 2 May 1967 this Phantom was lost during an aborted take-off due to fire at Cam Ranh Bay. (L. Wilson)

F-4C / 64-693
2nd AD / 45th TFS

Capt. Kenneth E. Holcombe
Capt. Ronald C. Anderson
Unknown 03

F-4C-22-MC 64-693 - Tail number 64-693 is pictured in this black and white photograph heading for a bombing mission in Northern Laos. F-4C 64-693 was the second Phantom involved in the 10 July 1965 MiG engagement that resulted in the first two Air Force MiG kills of the Vietnam War. Capts. Holcombe and Anderson downed their MiG with an AIM-9 missile. On 30 July 1967, while serving with the 12th TFW, 559th TFS, this F-4C was lost in combat over North Vietnam. (L. Wilson)

F-4C / 64-696
8th TFW / 555th TFS

Capt. William B. D. Dowell
1st Lt. Halbert E. Gossard
Unknown 03

F-4C-22-MC 64-696 - Being tasked with a MIGCAP mission on 29 April 1967, 64-696 was involved in an air battle that resulted in the destruction of a MIG 17. Fought in the area of the Bac Giang Bridge, 25 miles north of Hanoi, Capt. Dowell and Lt. Gossard downed their MiG with a Sidewinder. In this color photograph 64-696 is clearly armed for an air to ground mission some place in Southeast Asia. She is loaded with 750-pound bombs and an SUU-16 gun pod containing the M-61 Vulcan 20-mm cannon on the centerline of the aircraft. On 19 November 1967, while assigned to the 12th TFW, 559th TFS, this particular Phantom was lost in combat. (National Archives)

F-4C / 64-697
8th TFW / 555th TFS

Capt. Larry R. Keith
1st Lt. Robert A. Bleakley
Unknown 01

F-4C-22-MC 64-697 - This MiG killer is in line for refueling at Cam Ranh Bay, armed with Sidewinders and Sparrow missiles. Prior to her loss on 26 November 1967 over North Vietnam, Capt. Keith and Lt. Bleakley downed their MiG 17 by maneuvering the MiG into the ground on 29 April 1966. (National Archives)

F-4C / 64-699
8th TFW / 555th TFS

Capt. Robert E. Blake
1st Lt. S. W. George
Unknown 04

F-4C-22-MC 64-699 - Shown in the Tail Code "FP" of the 497th TFS out of Ubon RTAFB, 64-699 is being loaded with 750-pound iron bombs for a bombing mission in 1967. The red star trimmed in yellow appears on the splitter plate, noting her MiG kill. On 23 April 1966 Capt. Blake and Lt. George attacked and destroyed a MiG 17 with a Sparrow AIM-7 air-to-air missile. Blake states:

"I had a bad angle of attack on him and missed, but was able to realign and fire again. The second one connected."

In the second color photograph 64-699 has recently arrived at Davis Monthan AFB in 1989, bringing her service life to an end. (R. Picciani Collection / D. Erff)

F-4C / 64-720
8th TFW / 433rd TFS

Capt. John B. Stone
1st Lt. Clifton P. Dunnegan, Jr.
Rambler 01

F-4C-22-MC 64-720 - Another F-4 that is credited with a MiG 21 kill during "Operation Bolo." On 2 January 1967, flying as Rambler lead, Capt. Stone and Lt. Dunnegan took a flight of four MiG 21s under attack. Closing behind two MiGs, Stone fired three Sparrow missiles. One of the missiles detonated at the wing root of one of the enemy aircraft, successfully destroying it. The MiG pilot was seen to eject. In this color in-flight photograph 64-720 is armed with 500-pound iron bombs for another bombing mission in SEA. In 1967, 64-720 was lost during take off from Ubon RTAFB when ordnance on the aircraft exploded. (R Picciani Collection)

F-4C / 64-739
8th TFW / 433rd TFS

Maj. William L. Kirk
1st Lt. Stephen A. Wayne
Harpoon 01

F-4C-23-MC 64-739 - On 13 May 1967 Maj. Kirk and Lt. Wayne, of the 8th TFW, 433rd TFS, engaged, fired on, and destroyed a MiG 17. Their kill was one of seven MiG kills credited to Air Force F-4s and F-105s on 13 May 1967. Only the tail section of 64-739 is visible in this wartime photograph taken at the refueling pit at Cam Ranh Bay. This F-4C was lost in combat in South Vietnam on 25 January 1969 while assigned to the 557th TFS. (J. Stephan)

F-4D / 65-784
432nd TRW / 555th TFS

Maj. Roger A. Lodge
1st Lt. / Capt. Roger C. Locher
Falcon 62
Oyster 01

F-4D-29MC 65-784 - This F4D was credited with bringing down three MiG 21s during 1972. On 21 February '72, 8 May '72, and again on 10 May '72, this particular F-4D was flown by Maj. Lodge and Capt. Locher when they engaged, fired on, and destroyed three MiGs, all with AIM-7 missiles. After bringing down one MiG 21 with an AIM-7 missile during the 10 May '72 air battle, Maj. Lodge and Capt. Locher engaged a second MiG 21. They were taken under attack and shot down by a MiG 19 flown by Lt. Nguyen Manh Tung of the 925th Regiment of the Vietnamese Peoples' Air Force. Maj. Lodge was killed as a result of this action. Capt. Locher was able to eject from the damaged Phantom, and was rescued 23 days later deep within North Vietnam. Two very rare color photographs of 65-748 are presented here from the Patrick Martin Collection. Patrick Martin is a noted aviation historian, writer, and photographer from Canada. Photograph number one of 65-748 was taken on 22 April 1971 while assigned to the 391st TFS, 475th TFW, based at Misawa Air Base, Japan. This photograph was taken by Tadao Shibu Sawa. The second photograph of 65-748 was taken by Don Larsen as she appeared on 4 January 1972, at Udorn RTAFB. (P. Martin Collection)

F-4D / 65-796
432nd TRW / 4th TFS

Capt. Paul D. Howman
1st Lt. Lawrence W. Kullman
Crafty 01

F-4D-29-MC 65-796 - Shown here in the tail markings ("FA") of the 25th TFS, operating out of Ubon RTAFB. On 8 January '73 Capt. Howman and Lt. Kullman of the 432nd TRW were engaged in a MIGCAP mission when they downed a MiG 21 with an AIM-7 missile. This victory was the only USAF kill during 1973, and the last MiG kill of the Vietnam War. Col. James J. Crumbliss, USAF (Ret), took this in-flight photograph of F-4D 65-796 in the skies over SEA. At the time the photograph was taken she was assigned to the 25th TFS, based out of Ubon RTAFB. F-4D 65-796 survived the war, going on to serve with the 307th TFS, 31st TFW, at Homestead AFB, Florida. The second photograph of this historic Phantom presents her high on a pedestal in the Linear Air Park, Dyess AFB, Texas. (J. Crumbliss via D. Hansen)

F-4D / 65-801
432nd TRW / 555th TFS
Capt. Richard S. Ritchie
Capt. Lawrence H. Pettit
Icebag 01

F-4D-29-MC 65-801 - On 31 May '72, Capts. Ritchie and Pettit were flying as Icebag lead, along with four F-4s assigned to a MIGCAP mission northeast of Thai Nguyen. Capt. Pettit achieved a full system lock-on and fired four AIM-7 missiles. The fourth missile guided and impacted the forward fuselage section of the MIG. The MiG's front section broke off, and the aft section entered into a flat spin, impacting the ground. F-4D 65-801 appears in this John Sheets, April 1986 color photograph parked on the ramp of the 111th FIS, 147th FIG, based at Ellington AFB. (P. Martin Collection)

F-4D / 66-230
432nd TRW / 13th TFS
Capt. Frederick S. Olmsted Jr.
Capt. Gerald R. Volloy
Papa 01

F-4D-29-MC 66-230 - After being launched from Udorn RTAFB, Capts. Olmsted and Volloy were orbiting near the Laotian border when they were vectored by "Red Crown" to intercept an enemy aircraft. Olmsted and Volloy began engaging the MiG at a distance of 12 miles. After firing their third and last missile at approximately 4 miles, Captain Volloy states:

"A few seconds later both I and the aircraft commander, Capt. Olmsted, observed at 1 o'clock, almost level approximately 1-2 nautical miles ahead, a large reddish-yellow fireball that sustained itself for a few seconds."

F-4D 66-230 is depicted in this 12 January 1972 photograph while assigned to the 432nd TRW, 13th TFS, at Udorn. This F-4D was lost to an air-to-air missile during May 1972 over North Vietnam. (P. Martin Collection)

F-4D / 66-239
432nd TRW / 555th TFS

Capt. Calvin B. Tibbett
1st Lt. William S. Hardgrave
Olds 03

F-4D-29-MC 66-239 - On 9 September 1972, F-4s of the 555th TFS engaged in a MIGCAP mission were credited with bringing down three MiGs in air-to-air combat. Capt. Tibbett and Lt. Hardgrave downed a MiG 21...

"We closed to gun range and fired our 20-mm cannon. The enemy MiG sustained numerous hits along the fuselage and left wing. The MiG pilot was seen to eject."

In this 1984 photograph 66-239 is shown with the markings of the Kansas Air National Guard, based at McConnell AFB. (P. Martin Collection)

F-4D / 66-240
432nd TRW / 555th TFS

Capt. Gary L. Sholders
1st Lt. Eldon D. Binkley
Bucket 01

F-4D-29-MC 66-240 - Capt. Sholders and Lt. Binkley, flying as Bucket Lead, downed a MiG 21 after maneuvering the MiG into crashing approximately 60 miles west of Hanoi. In this post war photograph 66-240 is depicted in the markings of 31st TFW, 307th TFS, Homestead AFB, Florida. This particular photograph was taken at an Air National Guard Base in New Hampshire. (Author)

F-4D / 66-247
66-249
8th TFW / 555th TFS

Capt. Everett T. Raspberry Jr.
Capt. Francis M. Gullick
Drill 01

F-4D-29-MC 66-247

F-4D-29-MC 66-249 - During a MIGCAP mission in support of an Iron Hand flight in the vicinity of Thud Ridge, Capts. Raspberry and Gullick, flying as Drill lead, engaged, fired on, and destroyed a MiG 17 with an AIM-7 missile. This MiG kill was the first kill credited to an F-4D Phantom. Some question which of the two F-4Ds were flown by Raspberry and Gullick during their MiG kill mission of 5 June 1967. The day-to-day records of the 8th TFW identify the F-4 flown by Raspberry and Gullick as being F-4D-29-MC 66-249. Records further indicate that 66-249 was the first F-4D Phantom to bring down a MiG in air-to-air combat. There are numerous photographs of 66-249 marked as a MiG killer in the public records. However, in researching this project the author discovered in the document collection at the National Archives a MiG claim statement that was signed by Capt. Raspberry, identifying F-4D-29-MC 66-247 as the F-4D flown on 5 June '67. Lt. Col. Raspberry, USAF (Ret), has no present recollection of the correct tail number. With the similarity of the two tail numbers (66-247/66-249) the answer may be simply a typographical error. In any event, presented here are a series of outstanding photographs of both F-4Ds.

The first photograph is an in-flight photograph depicting 66-247 with the tail code "FY," which would identify her as being assigned to the 555th TFS at Ubon RTAFB at the time the photo-

graph was taken. On 23 August 1967, F-4D 66-247 was lost to an air-to-air missile over North Vietnam. (R. Picciani Collection)

The second photograph, by Frank MacSorley, was taken during 1967 of a well-worn 66-249. She is clearly marked on the splitter plate with the red star outlined in yellow, denoting a MiG 17 kill. (R. Picciani Collection)

Photographs three and four show 66-249 with the tail code "OY," indicating they may have been taken while she was assigned to the 432nd TRW, 555th TFS at Udorn RTAFB during 1971. In photograph number three 66-249 is armed with a load of MK 82 / 500 pound bombs. In the fourth photograph 66-249 is armed with cluster bombs and MK 82 / 500 pound bombs. (D. Larsen via P. Martin Collection)

The fifth photograph is a black and white Air Force photograph taken on 31 December 1967 of 66-249 being parked on the ramp at Udorn RTAFB while assigned to the 555th TFS (Triple Nickel). (USAF)

After surviving the war, this old warhorse was lost due to an in-flight fire over the Gulf of Mexico on 22 March 1985.

F-4D / 66-267
432nd TRW / 555th TFS

Capt. John A. Madden Jr.
Capt. Charles B. DeBellevue
Olds 01

F-4D-29-MC 66-267 - This was one of four F-4Ds on a MIGCAP mission in the area of Phuc Yen airfield. Olds flight was credited with downing three MiGs on 9 September 1972. Two MiG 19s fell victim to Captains Madden and DeBellevue, and were downed with AIM-9 missiles. The two kills were the first two for Captain Madden, but were the fifth and sixth for Captain DeBellevue. Two Red stars still appear on the splitter plate of 66-267 long after the Vietnam War. 66-267 is seen here in the markings of the wing commander of the 31st TFW during 1987. (P. Martin Collection)

F-4D / 66-268
432nd TRW / 555th TFS

Capt. John A. Madden Jr.
Capt. Lawrence H. Pettit
Vega 01

F-4D-29-MC 66-268 - On 12 October 1967, during Linebacker operations, Capts. Madden and Pettit, flying as Vega lead, detected two bandits airborne from Phuc Yen airfield heading northwest. Madden and Pettit, after aggressively attacking, were able to maneuver the MiG into crashing into the ground. Assigned to the 127th TFS, 184th TFG, Kansas Air National Guard, F-4D 66-268 is shown in these two photographs at the end of her service life. Note the leading edge flaps on the left wing are falling off as she is allowed to deteriorate. 66-268 was rescued and completely restored by the Combat Air Museum at Forbes Field, Topeka, Kansas. (R. Greby / T. Viens)

F-4D / 66-269
432nd TRW / 555th TFS

Lt. Col. James E. Brunson
Maj. Ralph S. Pickett
Buick 01

F-4D-29-MC 66-269 - While escorting strike aircraft in Route Package 6, Lt. Col. Brunson and Maj. Pickett fired four AIM-7 missiles in rapid succession:

"One of the AIM-7 missiles detonates in the tail section of the MiG 21, causing the tail section and large pieces...to separate. The MiG went into an uncontrollable spin."

In this photograph from the Patrick Martin collection, 66-269 was assigned to the 44th TFS, 18th TFW, at Kadena AB, Japan. The second photograph depicts 66-269 as she is today, on display at the Bradley Air Museum, Windsor Locks, Connecticut. (P. Martin Collection / Author)

F-4D / 66-271
432nd TRW / 13th TFS

Lt. Col. Carl G. Baily
Capt. Jeffrey S. Feinstein
Snug 01

F-4D-29-MC 66-271 - A MiG 21 fell victim to Lt. Col. Baily and Capt. Feinstein on 18 July '72. Baily and Feinstein were flying as Snug lead on a MIGCAP mission when they downed their MiG with an AIM-9 Sidewinder. Lt. Col. Baily and Capt. Feinstein claimed a second MiG kill on 29 July '72; when flying as Cadillac lead they down a MiG 21 in the area of Kep airfield. The second MiG was destroyed with an AIM-7 Sparrow missile. This black and white photograph depicting 66-271 with the "ZF" tail code was taken at Dobbins AFB, GA, on 27 April 1983. The color photograph shows 66-271 landing. At the time of the second photograph 66-271 was assigned to the 184th TFG, 127th FIS of the Kansas Air National Guard. (N. Taylor / F-4 Phantom Society)

F-4D / 66-274
8th TFW / 555th TFS

Capt. John D. Logeman Jr.
1st Lt. Frederick E. McCoy II
Ford 01

F-4D-29-MC 66-274 - While engaged in a MIGCAP flight for a photographic mission northwest of Phuc Yen airfield, Ford flight was jumped by six MiG 17s. In the air-to-air battle that followed American fighters downed three MiGs. One of the victories went to Capt. Logeman and Lt. McCoy, who were flying as Ford lead on 26 October 1967. Firing two AIM-7 missiles at an enemy MiG 17, the second missile was last seen on a collision course with the MiG. The enemy pilot was seen to eject by Ford lead and Ford 02. The 127th TFS, Kansas Air National Guard, operated this MiG killer long after the Vietnam War. 66-274 is presented here still in the Standard SEA camouflage color scheme, and with a red star on the splitter plate denoting her MiG kill of 26 October 1967. (P. Martin Collection)

F-4D / 66-280
432nd TRW / 523rd TFS

Capt. James C. Null
Capt. Michael D. Vahue
Papa 03

F-4D-29-MC 66-280 - On 16 April 1972 Capts. Null and Vahue were scrambled from Udorn RTAFB to investigate a possible hostile track. After the target had been declared hostile, Null and Vahue initiated an attack on the enemy aircraft. The MiG was downed with an AIM-7 Sparrow missile. F-4D 66-280 is pictured here in the markings of the 31st TFW. (P. Martin Collection)

F-4D / 66-7463
432nd. TRW / 555th TFS

Lt. Col. Joseph W. Kittinger
1st Lt. Leigh A. Hodgdon
01MAR72 MIG-21
Call SIGN: FALCON 54
TAIL CODE: OY
PRIMARY WEAPON: AIM-7

432nd. TRW - 13th TFS

Capt. Frederick S. Olmsted Jr.
Capt. Stuart W. Maas
16APR72 MIG-21
CALL SIGN: BASCO 01
TAIL CODE: OY
PRIMARY WEAPON: AIM-7

432nd TRW / 13th TFS

Maj. Barton P. Crews
Capt. Keith W. Jones
08MAY72 MIG-19
CALL SIGN: GALORE 03
TAIL CODE: OY
PRIMARY WEAPON: AIM-7

432nd TRW / 555th TFS

Capt. Richard S. Ritchie
Capt. Charles B. DeBellevue
10MAY72 MIG-21
CALL SIGN: OYSTER 03
Tail CODE: OY
PRIMARY WEAPON: AIM-7

432nd TRW / 555th TFS

Capt. Richard S. Ritchie
Capt. Charles B. DeBellvue
28AUG72 MIG-21
CALL SIGN: BUICK 01
TAIL CODE: OY
PRIMARY WEAPON: AIM-7

432nd / 523rd TFS

Maj. Ivy J. McCoy Jr.
Maj. Frederick W. Brown
15OCT72 MIG-21
CALL SIGN: CHEVY 01
TAIL CODE: OY
PRIMARY WEAPON: AIM-9

F-4D-29-MC 66-7463 - The only F-4 Phantom to claim "Ace" status during the Vietnam War. During 1972, F-4D 66-7463 destroyed six MiGs with six different aircrews. This particular Phantom further distinguished itself, in that it was the jet flown by Captain Richard S. Ritchie when he obtained "Ace" status on 28 August 1972. Only two other Phantom aircrew members would obtain "Ace" during the Vietnam War, Captains Charles B. DeBellevue and Jeffrey S. Feinstein.

On 8 May 1972 F-4D 66-7463 again distinguished itself when Major Barton P. Crews and Captain Keith W. Jones claimed the first MiG 19 kill of the Vietnam War. The engagements follow:

First MiG Kill: On 1 March 1972, Disco advised Falcon flight that MiGs were airborne in the area. Falcon 54, flown by Lt. Col. Kittinger and 1st Lt. Hodgdon, acquired the target and fired three AIM-7 missiles. The first two missiles failed to guide, but the third hit the mark, destroying the MiG. Lt. Col. Kittinger was himself shot down in another air battle just days after his March 1, 1972, victory. He was on his third tour of duty in Southeast Asia when downed.

Second MiG kill: Basco flight launched from Udorn RTAFB and proceeded to a pre-strike holding orbit:

"As we rolled out on a heading of 340-degrees, Captain Maas picked up two hostile aircraft indications on the radar scope, and at 20 nautical miles, Captain Maas made a radio call to my flight warning us of the danger."

Captains Olmsted and Maas visually identified the aircraft as hostile and engaged the MiGs. As a result of the air battle Captains Olmsted and Maas engaged a MiG 21, and fired on and destroyed the MiG with an AIM-7 missile.

Third MiG Kill: "They're not friendly!" Galore lead announced as he directed the engagement. Galore 03 (Maj. Crews and Capt. Jones) attacked an element of MiG 19s and were able to down one of them with an AIM-7 missile. This was the first MiG 19 kill credited to an F-4 Phantom during the Vietnam War.

Fourth MiG Kill: On 10 May '72 Oyster flight—a flight of Four F-4 Phantoms—while engaged in a MIGCAP mission in the area of Yen Bai, downed three MiG 21s. Oyster lead and Oyster 02 made initial contact with the enemy aircraft, and quickly downed two of the MiGs. Flying as Oyster 03, Ritchie and DeBellevue downed the third MiG of the air battle. Capt. Ritchie stated:

"We fired two Sparrow missiles at a MiG 21; the first passed just under the MiG, while the second guided perfectly and impacted the MiG."

Fifth MiG Kill: During a MIGCAP flight on 28 August 1972, Capt. Richard S. Ritchie became the United States Air Force's first confirmed "Ace" after he and Capt. DeBellevue downed a MiG 21 with an AIM-7 Sparrow missile.

Sixth MiG Kill: Flying in support of Linebacker missions, Majors McCoy and Brown of the 432nd TRW downed a MiG 21with an AIM-9 Sidewinder missile. "The entire aft section of the MiG 21 was a fireball and was disintegrating," reports Major McCoy.

The first two photographs of F-4D 66-7463 are from the personal collection of Donald Jay of North Carolina. Photograph number one was taken while 66-7463 was assigned to the 555th TFS during the late summer of 1972. Photograph number two is a nighttime photograph of 66-7463 taken in January or February 1973, while still assigned to the 555th TFS at Udorn RTAFB. (D. Jay Collection)

F-4D 66-7463 appears in this black and white photograph with the tail code "WP" while assigned to the 8th TFW, based at Osan Air Base, Korea. This particular photograph was taken at Clark Air Base, Philippines, on 30 March 1974 by D. Menard, and is from the Norm Taylor collection. (N. Taylor Collection)

In this October 1987, Douglas E. Slowiak photograph, 66-7463 is seen as she is today, preserved at the U.S. Air Force Academy, Colorado Springs, Colorado. She appears in the SEA camouflage color scheme as she did in 1972 during the Vietnam War. Proudly displayed on the splitter plate of 66-7463 are the six MiG kills that were credited to her during 1972. (D. Slowiak)

F-4D / 66-7468
432nd TRW / 555th TFS

Maj. Harry L. McKee
Capt. John E. Dubler
List 01

F-4D-29-MC 66-7468 - On 28 December 1972, while on a MIGCAP mission west of Hanoi, List flight downed a MiG 21. The bandit's location was called by Red Crown. Maj. McKee and Capt. Dubler promptly downed the MiG with an AIM-7 missile. In the third photograph presented, 66-7468 is seen on the ramp of the 170th TFS, 183rd TFG, based at Springfield, Illinois. She is still clearly marked as a MiG killer long after the Vietnam War. In the second photograph, taken at Udorn RTAFB, 66-7468 is marked with the red star of a MiG killer. She is fully loaded with a full complement of Sparrow and Sidewinder missile for a MIGCAP mission. In the first photograph 66-7468 is high on her pedestal at the home of the 183rd TFG, Springfield, Illinois. (P. Martin Collection / D. Jay / Public Affairs Office, 183rd TFG)

DY
468

SI
468
468

F-4D / 66-7501
432nd TRW / 13th TFS

Lt. Col. Curtis D. Westphal
Capt. Jeffrey s. Feinstein
Olds 01

F-4D-30-MC 66-7501- During a MIGCAP mission on 13 October 1972, Captain Jeffrey S. Feinstein became the third Air Force pilot to obtain "Ace" status. Flying as the WSO with Lt. Col. Westphal, they engaged one of two MiG 21s in the vicinity of Hanoi. The AIM-7 Sparrow missile was observed to strike the aft section of the MiG, bursting it into flames. F-4D 66-7501 is seen in this unique color photograph high above the clouds, taking on fuel for a bombing mission somewhere in SEA. In the black and white photograph 66-7501 is assigned to the 480th TFS, 12th TFW, based at Phu Cat AB, Vietnam. The aircraft is armed with six 500-pound high drag bombs and four napalm tanks. The photo was taken as the aircraft was departing the revetment area on 10 September 1970. This MiG killer was lost in Vietnam on 20 November 1972. (J. Crumbliss / N. Taylor Collection)

F-4D / 66-7546
8th TFW / 555th TFS

Capt. William S. Gordon III
1st Lt. James H. Monsees
Ford 03

F-4D-30-MC 66-7546 - During a MIGCAP flight for a photographic mission four F-4Ds of Ford flight were jumped by six MiG 17s. As a result of the air battle, a total of three enemy MiG 17s were downed by air-to-air missiles. One of the MiGs was brought down by Capt. Gordon and Lt. Monsees with an AIM-7 Sparrow missile. On 1 October 1962 F-4D 66-7546 was lost in combat to 37mm anti-aircraft fire over Laos. In this Vietnam era photograph of 66-7546 she is loaded with 500 pound MK 82 bombs and two cluster weapons. (D. Jay Collection)

F-4D / 66-7550
432nd TRW / 13th TFS

Maj. Edward D. Cherry
Capt. Jeffery S. Feinstein
Basco 03

F-4D-30-MC 66-7550 - As part of Basco flight, on 16 April 1972 Maj. Cherry and Capt. Feinstein engaged, fired on, and destroyed a MiG 21 in air-to-air combat. Major Cherry's account:

"I fired one AIM-7 radar missile that impacted the MiG 21 just aft of the right wing post. The MiG's right wing immediately separated, and the aircraft went into a wild, gyrating spin to the left, trailing smoke and aircraft fragments."

In photograph one, F-4D 66-7550 is caught at the moment of lift off armed with 500 pound MK 82 bombs for another mission in SEA. In the second photograph she has been preserved after service with the 89th TFS of the Ohio Air National Guard. (P. Martin Collection / Author)

F-4D / 66-7554
8th TFW / 555th TFS

Maj. Rex D. Howerton
1st Lt. Ted L. Voigt II
Nash 03

F-4D-30-MC 66-7554 - The MiGs were maneuvering in a left hand Wagon Wheel maneuver northwest of Phuc Yen when they were engaged by Maj. Howerton and Lt. Voigt. In the words of Maj. Howerton:

"Cannon hits were noted on the MiG, and shortly thereafter the MiG exploded and began to break up."

F-4D 66-7554 is seen in this Vietnam era photograph with the tail code markings of the 555th TFS. Clearly present on the splitter plate of this F-4D are two red stars, which indicate that she has downed two MiGs. Though marked as a double MiG killer since the Vietnam era, official records only indicate that she downed the one MiG 17 on 14 February 1968 when flying as a member of Nash flight. The second photograph of 66-7554 is taken well after the Vietnam War while serving with the 89th TFS, 906th TFG of the Ohio Air National Guard. Note the splitter plate displays three MiG kills. The final series of photographs depicts 66-7554 high on a pedestal at Wright Patterson AFB, Ohio, where she has been preserved. (P. Martin Collection / History Office Wright Patterson AFB / Author)

DO
554

DO
AF
66 554

F-4D / 66-7565
8th TFW / 555th TFS

Capt. Larry D. Cobb
Capt. Alan A. Lavoy
Ford 04

F-4D-30-MC 66-7565 - The third MiG claimed by Ford flight on 26 October 1967 was credited to Captains Cobb and Lavoy, who downed a MiG 17 with an AIM-4D Falcon missile. The aircraft commander said:

"I observed the AIM-4D impact on the tail of the MiG 17, and explosion; the MiG started to roll right and spiral earthward in flames. "

In this period photograph, 66-7565 is being readied in the revetment area for another combat mission. This 555th TFS Phantom was lost in combat over North Vietnam on 17 August 1968. In this photograph 66-7565 is armed with MK 82 500-pound bombs. (M. Druzolowski via P. Schinkelshoek)

F-4D / 66-7594
8th TFW / 435th TFS

Lt. Col. Clayton K. Squier
1st LT. Michael D. Muldoon
Olds 01

F-4D-30-MC 66-7594 - After a strike on the Trung Quang railroad yard, Olds flight was egressing the target area when they were attacked by a force of MiG 17s. In the ensuing air battle Olds lead, crewed by Lt. Col. Squier and Lt. Muldoon, took under attack one of the MiG 17s:

"The missile tracked directly to the aft section of the MiG and impacted in a ball of fire and smoke."

Left side view of aircraft 66-7594 showing its MiG 17 kill markings. The aircraft was assigned to the 435th TFS, 8th TFW, based at Ubon RTAFB. This photograph was taken at Phu Cat Air Base, Vietnam, on 19 September by Norm Taylor. (N. Taylor Collection)

F-4D / 66-7601
8th. TFW / 435th TFS

Capt. Darrell D. Simmonds
1st Lt. George H. McKinney Jr.
Sapphire 01

Maj. Joseph D. Moore
1st Lt. George H. McKinney Jr.
Nash 01

F-4D-30-MC 66-7601 - The first MiG warnings came while the Iron Hand flight was coming off the target after a Shrike [AGM-45 air-to-ground radar-seeking missile] launch. Sapphire lead, Capt. Simmonds and Lt. McKinney, initially made contact with the MiGs as they were attacking the egressing flights of strike aircraft. As a result of taking the MiGs under attack, Capt. Simmonds and Lt. McKinney engaged the MiGs in an old fashioned dogfight, downing two of the MiG 17s with 20-mm cannon fire. On 19 December 1967 the aircrew of Maj. Moore and Lt. McKinney claimed a third MiG kill in F-4D 66-7601. Flying as Nash lead, they engaged a MiG 17 that was attacking a flight of F-105 strike aircraft. Moore and McKinney observed smoke coming from the MiG's fuselage. Nash lead was being closed on by another MiG 17 and was forced to unload and accelerate away.

As a result of review by the 7th Air Force MiG Claims Evaluation Board, Maj. Joseph D. Moore and 1st Lt. George H. McKinney, Jr., received credit for only one-half of a MiG kill. The other half was awarded to an F-105F (tail number 63-8329) aircrew from the 355th. TFW, 333rd TFS; Majors William M. Dalton, pilot, and James L. Graham, EWO, were part of an Iron Hand mission. During a combat mission over North Vietnam on 18 February 1972 this Phantom was lost to a surface-to-air missile. F-4D 66-7601 is depicted in this beautiful photograph taken on 24 August 1967 by Don Larsen, while she was assigned to the 435th TFS, 8th TFW at Ubon RTAFB. In this photograph 66-7601 is fully loaded with cluster bombs. In the second photograph, which depicts the cockpit area of 66-7601, you can clearly see the splitter plate with the two and one-half MiG kills. The red stars are trimmed in white. (P. Martin Collection / J. Velten)

RESCUE

F-4D / 66-7661
8th TFW / 435th TFS
432nd TRW / 555th TFS

Col. David O. Williams Jr.
1st Lt. James P. Feighny Jr.
Killer 01

Capt. Stephene E. Nichols
1st Lt. James R. Bell
Gopher 02

F-4D-31-MC 66-7661 - During an air-to-air battle, an F-4D of the 435th TFS downed a MiG 17 over the flats northeast of Phuc Yen. During the air battle, Killer lead's Col. Williams and Lt. Feighny downed a MiG 17 with an AIM-7 missile. In the second aerial victory credited to 66-7661 the kill was awarded two years after the air battle.

"On 15 July 1974, Pacific Air Force (PACAF) awarded credit for the aerial victory to Capt. Stephen E. Nichols, aircraft commander, and 1st Lt. James R. Bell, weapon systems officer, of the 'Triple Nickel' squadron."

Flying as Gopher 02, Nichols and Bell downed their MiG 21 on 11 May 1972 with an AIM-7 Sparrow missile. In this in-flight Norman L. Komnick photograph, 66-7661 is part of a flight of Phantoms from the 8th TFW, 435th TFS. Although only marked with one MiG kill, she is credited with downing two MiGs during the war. This excellent photograph of 66-7661 was obtained from the Ron Picciani Collection. The next post war photograph depict 66-7661 on the ramp of the 113th TFW, Andrews Air Force Base, Maryland. She appears in two-tone gray camouflage. After her service with the 113th TFG, 66-7661 was retired to a pedestal in front of the Air National Guard Building at Andrews AFB, as displayed in this series of color photographs. (R. Picciani Collection / Author)

DC
AF 66 661

DC
AF 66 661

F-4D / 66-7748
8th TFW / 433rd TFS

Maj. Bernard J. Bogoslofski
Capt. Richard L. Huskey
Tampa 01
No Photo Available

F-4D-31-MC 66-7748 - Maj. Bogoslofski and his back seater, Capt. Huskey, were flying the lead aircraft in Tampa flight on 3 January 1968 when they witnessed an attack by a MiG 17 on a flight of F-4s. Bogoslofski and Huskey initiated a gun attack on the MiG 17. Bogoslofski reported:

" A burst of fire appeared on the MiG's left wing, and fragmentation of the aircraft's left wing was observed."

Tampa 04 saw the pilot eject, and the MiG hit the ground. Many attempts have been made to obtain a photograph of F-4D 66-7748, but have met with little success. However, there is at least one photograph of this particular Phantom that appears on page 45 of the book *MiG Kill Markings from the Vietnam War* by Bert Kinzey and Ray Leader. On 4 November 1969, while assigned to the 8th TFW, 497th TFS, F-4D 66-7748 was lost in combat in Southeast Asia.

F-4D / 66-7750
8th TFW / 433rd TFS

Maj. William I. Kirk
1st Lt. Theodore R. Bongartz
Buick 01

F-4D-31-MC 66-7750 - On 24 October 1967 Maj. Kirk and Bongartz, who were on a MIGCAP mission during a raid of Phuc Yen, engaged a MiG 21. Kirk and Bongartz fired two AIM-7 missiles at the MiG, but failed to down the enemy aircraft. They switched to guns and started firing:

"I could see large pieces coming off of the fuselage, and the entire fuselage section was engulfed in flames."

Sitting on the ramp in this black and white photograph, 66-7750 reflects the markings of the 465th TFS, 507th TFG AFRES at Tinker AFB. (J. Geer Collection)

F-4D / 66-8688
8th TFW / 433rd TFS

Capt. Robert H. Boles
1st Lt. Robert B. Bettista
Buick 04

F-4D-31-MC 66-8688 - Capt. Boles and Lt. Bettista "...after several MiG calls, turned into the threat and engaged two MiG 21s." One of the MiG 21s was downed with an AIM-7 Sparrow missile. Capt. Boles states:

"The missile detonated at the left aft wing root section, and the MiG exploded."

F-4D 66-8688 is shown in this Richard Kierbow, in-flight photograph heading north on another combat mission. The tail code "FG" identifies her as being assigned to the 433rd TFS when this photograph was taken. (R. Kierbow / JEM Aviation Slides)

F-4D / 66-8690
8th TFW / 435th TFS

Lt. Col. Alfred E. Lang Jr.
1st Lt. Randy P. Moss
Buick 01

F-4D-31-MC 66-8690 - Buick flight was one of two MIGCAP flights protecting strike aircraft attacking the Cao Nung railroad yard. While withdrawing from the target area, Buick lead's Lt. Col. Lang and Lt. Moss sighted two bogies at their 9 o'clock position. Buick lead was able to successfully engage one of the MiG 21s, and downed it with two Sparrow missiles. In this Robert Leavitt wartime photograph, 66-8690 is parked on the ramp of the 433rd TFS at Ubon RTAFB after completing a combat mission in SEA. (R. Leavitt / via D. Slowiak; Vortex Photo)

F-4D / 66-8714
432nd TRW / 13th TFS

Capt. Robert G. Hill
1st Lt. Bruce V. Huneke
Gambit 03

F-4D-32-MC 66-8714 - Gambit 03 (Capt. Hill and Lt. Huneke) were part of a MIGCAP flight tasked with protecting a strike force that was attacking the Thai Nguyen area. The F-105 strike flight was attacked by MiGs, which resulted in the loss of one of the Thuds. Hill and Huneke engaged one of the attacking MiG 21s and downed it with an AIM-4 Falcon missile. Capt. Hill reports:

"The MiG exploded in a large red fireball of flame, blowing off the tail section."

In this July 1980, Pat Martin photograph, 66-8714 is seen during her take off roll from Greenham Common RAF, England. The tail code "SP" indicates that she is assigned to the 23rd TFS, 52ndnd TFW. (P. Martin Collection)

F-4D / 66-8719
432nd TRW / 13th TFS

Capt. Doyle D. Baker (USMC)
1st Lt. John D. Ryan Jr.
Gambit 03

F-4D-32-MC 66-8719 - A United States Marine Corps exchange pilot, Capt. Doyle D. Baker, and his back seater, Lt. John D. Ryan, teamed up to down a MiG 21 on 12 December 1967. The action took place in North Vietnam in the area of Phuc Yen airfield. Baker and Ryan downed the MiG with an AIM-4 Falcon missile. F-4D 66-8719 sits in the revetment at Udorn RTAFB, waiting to be armed for another combat mission. (P. Martin Collection)

F-4D / 66-8720
8th TFW / 435th TFS

Maj. Kenneth A. Simonet
1st Lt. Wayne O. Smith
Otter 01
No Photo Available

F-4D-32-MC 66-8720 - Maj. Simonet and Lt. Smith observed a MiG 17 as they came off the target; they cooled an AIM-4 missile and fired at the MiG. The missile was observed making contact, and exploding in the MiG's tail pipe. After downing the MiG, Simonet and Smith were shot down by an enemy MiG. Both were able to eject from their heavily damaged Phantom, and were captured and remained POWs till war's end.

F-4D / 66-8734
432nd TRW / 555th TFS

1st Lt. John D. Markle
Capt. Stephen D. Eaves
Oyster 02

F-4D-32-MC 66-8734 - Oyster 03 (Lt. Markle and Capt. Eaves) engaged a MiG 21 that was a threat to Oyster flight. Oyster flight was tasked as a MIGCAP flight on 10 May 1972 when the action took place. Markle and Eaves destroyed their MiG with an AIM-7 missile. In this period photograph of 66-8734 she is being readied for a ground support mission. She appears to be loaded with cluster bomb dispensers. (P. Martin Collection)

F-4D / 66-8756
432nd TRW / 555th TFS

Lt. Col. Wayne T. Frye
Lt. Col. James P. Cooney
Harlow 02

F-4D-32-MC 66-8756 - On 12 May 1972 Harlow flight (Lt. Col. Frye and Lt. Col. Cooney) were on a MIGCAP mission northwest of Yen Bai airfield when they engaged a MiG 19 in a low level (500-1,000 feet) air battle. In the ensuing air battle they downed the MiG 19 with an AIM-7 missile. Frye and Cooney were the first two Lieutenant Colonels in the same fighter to down a MiG, and coincidently, they were also the oldest aircrew to claim a MiG, with Frye being 41 years old and Cooney 44 years old at the time. In this war time photograph taken on 2 December '73 (from the Don Jay collection), 66-8756 is assigned to the 13th TFS, 432nd TRW. The second photograph of 66-8756 is a post war photograph while assigned to the 457th TFS, AFRES, based at Carswell AFB, Texas. (D. Jay Collection / P. Martin Collection)

F-4E / 66-313
388th TFW / 34th TFS

Capt. Charles D. Barton
1st Lt. George D. Watson
Eagle 04

F-4E-32-MC 66-313 - Two F-4 aircrews of the 34th TFS joined for an unusual MiG 19 kill. On 6 October 1972 Capt Barton and Lt. Watson, flying F-4E tail number 66-313, and Maj. Clouser and Lt. Burnson, flying F-4E tail 67-392, became involved in an air battle in the area of Thai Nguyen. During the battle the MiG 19 pilot:

"...apparently became so engrossed with the chase that he failed to notice the vertical dive angle until it was too late. His MiG impacted with the ground."

This in-flight photograph of 66-313 is the first in a series of outstanding F-4E photographs taken by Don Logan. Don Logan was an F-4E crewmember, and during 1972 flew 133 combat missions in SEA. (D. Logan Collection)

F-4E / 67-210
432nd TRW / 58th TFS

Maj. Philip W. Handley
1st Lt. John J. Smallwood
Brenda 01

F-4E-33-MC 67-210 - More than 250 American aircraft were involved in air strikes in North Vietnam on 2 June 1972. The attack was designed to disrupt supply and transportation systems. Maj. Handley and Lt. Smallwood engaged a MiG 19 in air-to-air combat while they were escorting the strike aircraft, and destroyed the MiG with 20-mm cannon fire. The MiG was observed to trail smoke from the left wing root before crashing into a green meadow. In this outstanding Richard Kierbow, in-flight photograph, 67-210 is fitted with electronic countermeasure equipment and Sidewinder missiles for a mission over North Vietnam. In this photograph 67-210 is accompanied by an F-4D from the 555th TFS, 432nd TRW. In the second color photograph—now marked as a MiG killer—66-210 is readied for another combat mission. In this photograph she is fitted with what appears to be 750-pound bombs. (R. Kierbow / and F-4 Phantom Society)

F-4E / 67-232
432nd TRW / 307th TFS

Capt. Gray M. Rubus
Capt. James L. Hendrickson
Buick 03

F-4E-34-MC 67-232 - Buick flight was flying MIGCAP for a Linebacker mission when they engaged, fired on, and destroyed a MiG 21. Capts. Rubus and Hendrickson were flying northwest of Bullseye (Hanoi) when they were vectored to intercept two MiG 21s. Upon contact they engaged the MiG with their 20mm cannon:

"Both bursts impacted the MiG, and shortly thereafter I observed the pilot eject."

In this view of 67-232 she is in the tail code markings of the 308th TFS, 31st TFW, Homestead Air Force Base. At the time the photograph was taken in October 1972, 67-232 was TDY to Udorn RTAFB. This particular photograph was taken in the skies over Laso. (R. Kierbow Collection)

F-4E / 67-239
432nd TRW / 58th TFS

Capt. Lawrence G. Richard (USMC)
Lt. CDR. Michael J. Ettel (USN)
Dodge 01

F-4E-34-MC 67-239 - On 12 August 1972 Capt. Richard and Lt. CDR. Ettel were exchange pilots with the 58th TFS when they downed a MiG 21 with an AIM-7 missile. The missile impacted the MiG just forward of the vertical fin. In this Mike France photograph 67-239 is painted in the Southeast Asia camouflage scheme. The photograph was taken at an airbase in England. This particular F-4E was sold to Egypt and is now serving with the Egyptian Air Force. (M. France Collection)

F-4E / 67-268
388th TFW / 35th TFS

Maj. Gary L. Retterbush
1st Lt. Daniel L. Autrey
Finch 03

F-4E-34-MC 67-268 - A flight of four F-4Es downed two MiG 21s while escorting a chaff flight in the vicinity of Kep airfield. Finch 03 (Maj. Retterbush and Lt. Autrey) downed one of the MiGs. After attempts failed with both AIM-7 and AIM-9 missiles to bring down the enemy aircraft, Finch 03 switched to guns. Retterbush stated;

"The 20-mm with tracers was observed impacting the fuselage, wing, and canopy, causing fire and smoke."

F-4E 67-268 is seen in this color photograph over northeast Thailand or Laos with a full complement of 500-pound MK 82 bombs. The photograph was taken sometime in June 1971 by Captain Richard Kierbow, who was a KC-135 aircraft commander with over 380 combat missions, over 100 in tankers. (R. Kierbow / JEM Aviation)

F-4E / 67-270
366th TFW / 4th TFS

Capt. Richard F. Hardy
Capt. Paul T. Lewinski
Brenda 03

F-4E-34-MC 67-270 - "Red Crown warned that bandits were attacking." One of the MiGs was engaged by Brenda 03, Capts. Hardy and Lewinski. The first AIM-7 they fired was a direct hit. The exploding missile caused the right wing to be blown off, and the enemy jet tumbled end over end. The black and white photograph, from the collection of aviation historian and photographer Jerry Geer, depicts 66-270 in the markings of the 21st TFTS of the Georgia Air National Guard with two MiG kills. The second photograph depicts 66-270 after completing her service life with the 108th TFW, McGuire AFB, New Jersey, still marked with two MiG kills. The dates for the two kills are listed as 8 July 1972 and 29 July 1972. However, the only documented kill (29 July 1972) is credited to another F-4E, tail number 67-292. (J. Geer Collection / Author)

F-4E / 67-275
388th TFW / 35th TFS

Lt. Col. Lyle L. Beckers
1st Lt. Thomas M. Griffin
Finch 01

F-4E-34-MC 67-275 - "We pursued the MiG and fired two AIM-9 missiles, one of which impacted the MiG's left wing." The left wing of the MiG was observed in flames. Beckers and Griffin then dove on the MiG and finished it off with their 20-mm cannon, firing some 520 rounds. A number of tracer rounds were observed to hit the MiG, causing additional damage. In this color photograph of 66-275 in the revetment area, she looks like a hungry shark looking for another MiG meal. (D. Logan Collection)

F-4E / 67-281
366th TFW / 35th TFS

Lt. Col. Lyle L. Beckers
Capt. John F. Huwe
Balter 01

F-4E-34-MC 67-281 - During an engagement with eight MiGs on 23 May 1972, Lt. Col. Beckers and Capt. Huwe destroyed a MiG 19 with an AIM-7 Sparrow missile. They were in the area of Kep airfield, assigned to protect a chaff flight when the air battle took place. In this photograph by Captain Tom Wallace, 67-281 is assigned to the 421st TFS, 366TFW. This particular photograph was taken at Clark AFB, Philippines. (P. Martin Collection)

F-4E / 67-283
388th TFW / 469th TFS

Lt. Col. Von R. Christiansen
Maj. Kaye M. Harden
Iceman 03

F-4E-35-MC 67-283 - While escorting a chaff-dispensing aircraft on 21 June 1972, Iceman 03 (Lt. Col. Christiansen and Major Harden), of the 469th TFS, engaged in an air battle with a flight of MiG 21s. Lt. Col. Christiansen reported:

"Major Harden observed the second missile guide directly into the MiG's tail, causing the MiG to explode and burn fiercely from the canopy aft,"

In this excellent Don Logan, in-flight photograph, 67-283 is on the wing of another Phantom, heading home with empty bomb racks. (D. Logan Collection)

F-4E / 67-292
366th TFW / 4th TFS

Lt. Col. Gene E. Taft
Capt. Stanley M. Imaye
Pistol 01

F-4E-35-MC 67-292 - While on an escort mission deep into North Vietnam, Pistol flight came under attack by surface-to-air missile and MiGs. Pistol lead (Lt. Col. Taft and Capt. Imaye) engaged a MiG 21 and destroyed the MiG with an AIM-7 missile. The MiG was observed to burn and roll uncontrollably. F-4E 67-0292 is shown in this December 1972, Harley Copic color photograph while serving at Udorn RTAFB, Thailand. A red star denoting a MiG 21 victory appears prominently on the nose of the aircraft. On 27 December 1972, F-4E 66-292 was lost in an air engagement with a MiG over North Vietnam. (H. Copic Collection)

F-4E / 67-301
388th TFW / 34th TFS

Maj. Robert L. Holtz
1st Lt. William C. Diehl
Parrot 03

F-4E-35MC 67-301 - Numerous MiGs were engaged during an air battle in the area of Viet Tri on 15 October 1972. Flying as Parrot 03, Maj. Holtz and Lt. Diehl engaged a MiG 21 and successfully destroyed the MiG with an AIM-9 Sidewinder missile. Holts stated:

"I fired an AIM-9 that came off the rail, did a slow roll, and then went straight up the MiG's tail and exploded, blowing pieces of tail section and almost one complete elevator off of the aircraft."

F-4E 67-301 appears in this in-flight photograph in the markings of the 388th TFW. This aircraft scored the last MiG kill of the war for the 388th TFW while at Korat RTAFB. (D. Logan Collection)

F-4E / 67-333
366th TFW / 35th TFS

Capt. James M. Beatty Jr.
1st Lt. James M. Summer
Balter 03

F-4E-35-MC 67-333 - Capt. Beatty and Lt. Sumner attacked a MiG 21 on 23 May 1972. While operating as Blater 03, Blater flight became involved in a battle with eight MiGs. During the course of the battle, Beatty and Sumner downed their MiG with their aircraft's 20-mm cannon. In his MiG claim statement Beatty reported:

"I estimate that I put 50-100 rounds in him, and his plane began to come apart and roll to the left."

F-4E 67-333 is pictured in this Don Jay photograph in the revetment area at Da Nang Air Base, Vietnam, in July 1971. In the black and white photograph 67-333 is shown landing at Phu Cat Air Base, Vietnam, on 19 June 1972. The "LC" tail code identifies her as being assigned to the 421st TFS, 366th TFW, based at Da Nang. (D. Jay Collection / N. Taylor Collection)

F-4E / 67-362
432nd TRW / 555th TFS

Capt. Richard S. Ritchie
Capt. Charles B. DeBellevue
Paula 01

F-4E-36-MC 67-362 - On 8 July 1972 Capts. Ritchie and DeBellevue were flying lead in a MIGCAP flight west of Phu Tho when they were informed by both Disco and Red Crown that enemy aircraft were in the area. In the air engagement that took place Capts. Ritchie and DeBellevue downed two MiG 21s with AIM-7 missiles. Both MiGs were observed to explode in large yellow fireballs. Long after the war 67-362 is still painted in the SEA camouflage color scheme while serving with the 58th TFS, 33rd TFW. (J. Geer Collection)

F-4E / 67-392
388th TFW / 34th and 35th TFS

Maj. Jon I. Lucas
1st Lt. Douglas G. Malloy
Eagle 03
Maj. Gordon L. Clouser

1st Lt. Cecil H. Brunson
Eagle 03

F-4E-36-MC 67-392 - Eagle flight was on a SAM suppression mission in the area of Phuc Yen airfield when Eagle 02 was attacked by a MiG 19. Maj. Lucas and Lt. Malloy were able to maneuver into position and down the MiG with an air-to-air missile. On 6 October 1972 Maj. Clouser and Lt. Brunson, flying as Eagle 04, joined with another Phantom aircrew to bring down a MiG 19. The two Phantoms were able to maneuver the MiG into crashing.

"Bombs Away" - In this in-flight photograph 67-393 is depicted releasing a load of 500-pound MK 82 bombs from her multiple ejector racks some place over Vietnam. Note the forward bombs are equipped with fuse extenders. In the third post war photograph 67-392 sits on the ramp at Travis Field, Savannah, Georgia, the two MiG 19 kills still displayed on the splitter plate. The final photograph of this Phantom was taken of her at the Virginia Air and Space Center. (D. Logan / E. Munsell / P. Schlink)

MY
392

JJ
392

F-4E / 68-338
432nd TRW / 13th TFS

Capt. Bruce G. Leonard Jr.
Capt. Jeffery S. Feinstein
Gopher 03

432nd. TRW / 555th TFS

Capt. Calvin B. Tibbett
1st Lt. William S. Hargrove
Chevy 03

F-4E-37-MC 68-338 - While Air Force strike fighters engaged targets near Kep airfield, their MIGCAP flight was engaged in a heated air battle with a number of MiG 21s. Gopher 03 (Capts. Leonard and Feinstein) engaged, fired on, and destroyed a MiG 21 with an AIM-9 Sidewinder missile. On 16 September 1972 Capts. Tibbett and Lt. Hargrove, while engaged in Linebacker operations, downed a MiG 21. The missile guided and detonated near the aft portion of the fuselage. Tibbett stated, "The MiG pilot ejected just before impact." F-4E 68-338 is shown in this Pat Martin color photograph in the tail code "WA," identifying her as being assigned to the 414th Fighter Weapons Squadron, 57th Fighter Weapons Wing at Nellis AFB, Nevada. 68-338 is seen in the European color scheme with black tail code and tail number. In the second photograph 68-338 is deployed to Travis Air National Guard Base in Georgia during Operation Quick Trust. At the time the photos were taken she was assigned to the 110th TFS, 131st TFW, Missouri Air National Guard. (P. Martin /Author)

F-4E / 68-493
388th TFW / 34th TFS

Capt. Richard E. Coe
1st Lt. Omri K. Webb III
Robin 01

F-4E-40-MC 68-493 - On 5 October 1972 Robin flight became involved in a heated battle when MiGs from Kep airfield attacked an Air Force strike force. During the air battle, Capt. Coe and Lt. Webb destroyed a MiG 21 with an AIM-7 missile. In this October 1972 photograph, 68-493 is seen in formation with 68-431. Both aircraft are loaded with Sidewinder and Sparrow missiles. The absence of external fuel tanks may be an indication of a recent MiG encounter. Note the red star on the splitter plate of 68-493 recognizing her MiG kill of 5 October 1972. (R. Kierbow Collection)

F-4E / 69-276
366th TFW / 35th TFS

Maj. Gray L. Retterbush
Capt. Robert H. Jasperson
Lark 01

F-4E-42-MC 69-276 - Lark flight was on a strike escort mission on 8 October 1972 when they encountered MiGs. Lark lead (Maj. Retterbush and Capt. Jasperson) attempted to down a MiG 21 with an AIM-9 missile that failed to fire. Switching to the aircraft's 20-mm cannon, they pressed the attack. They hit the MiG and observed as it burst into flames. F-4E 69-276 is seen hitting the tanker on its way to another combat mission. Within just a few days (12 October 1972) of this MiG kill 69-276 fell victim to an air-to-air missile from an enemy MiG. In this photograph 69-276 appears to be loaded with 500 pound MK 82 bombs. (D. Logan Collection)

F-4E / 69-291
388th TFW / 4th TFS

Capt. Sammy C. White
1st Lt. Frank J. Bettine
Pistol 03

F-4E-42-MC 69-291 - During his last Linebacker mission, Capt. White and his backseater, Lt. Bettine, downed a MiG 21. After obtaining position on the MiG, they fired an AIM-7 that struck the MiG. The pilot of the MiG was seen to eject from his smoking and burning aircraft. 69-291 is shown in this period photograph parked in the revetment area being readied for a bombing mission. In this photograph 69-291 is armed with MK 82 500-pound bombs. Note the white silhouette on the splitter plate denoting her MiG kill of 19 August 1972. This Phantom is now on display at Osan Air Base, South Korea. (R. Wilkie / USAF Osan AB; for the Author)

F-4E / 69-7235
8th TFW / 366th TFS

Capt. Fred W. Sheffler
Capt. Mark A. Massen
Date 04

F-4E-43-MC 69-7235 - On 15 August 1972, while on a chaff-dispensing mission, Capts. Sheffler and Massen tangled with a MiG 21. As a result of the ensuing air battle, Sheffler and Massen downed a MiG 21 with a radar missile.

"The missile made two minor corrections in flight: one just prior to impact on the left side, just forward of the tail section."

In this black and white photograph from the Jerry Geer collection, 69-7235 is seen on the ramp being readied for a flight. In this photograph 69-7235 is in the tail markings of the 347th Fighter Wing, Moody Air Force Base, Georgia. (J. Geer)

MiG Killers F-105s

F-105D / 58-1156 388th TFW / 421st TFS

Maj. Fred Tracy Crab 02

F-105D-5-RE 58-1156 - On 29 June '66 Maj. Fred Tracy, of the 388th TFW, 421st TFS, claimed the first MiG kill in an F-105 Thunderchief. During the air battle Maj. Tracy was attacked by a MiG 17.

"One 23-mm slug entered the cockpit and knocked Tracy's hand off the throttle, putting him out of afterburner and damaging his instruments, including his gun sight. The MiG overshot Tracy's aircraft and ended up at Tracy's 12 o'clock position."

Major Tracy was then able to take the MiG under attack:

"I fired 200 rounds of 20-mm, observing about 10 hits. The MiG rolled over and did a Split-S into the clouds at an altitude of 2000 feet."

F-105D 58-1156 is depicted in this Ken Kerering 29 June 1966 color photograph showing the exit hole of one of the 23-mm rounds that hit Tracy's aircraft during the air battle. Lt. Karl W. Richter,

421st TFS, is seen in this black and white photograph exiting the cockpit of 58-1156, holding what appears to be a bottle of champagne, celebrating the completion of his 100th mission. All eviden suggests that this is a publicity photograph, aka a "Tiger" shot, as Lt. Richter flew his 100th mission in F-105D 59-1766, not 58-1156. The purpose of displaying this photograph is to show 58-1156 (Maj. Tracy's kill of 29 June '66) marked as a MiG killer. However, Lt. Richter also claimed a MiG kill in F-105D 59-1766 on 21 September 1966. F-105D 58-1156 was lost to hostile fire on 21 January 1967 that forced her to crash into the sea. (K. Kerering / J. Kolla)

F-105D / 58-1168
355th TFW / 354th TFS

Maj. Jack W. Hunt
Nitro 01

F-105D-5-RE 58-1168 - Nitro flight was originally tasked to attack the Xuan Mai Army barracks in North Vietnam when they were jumped by a flight of MiG 17s. In the ensuing air battle Nitro lead, Nitro 2, and Nitro 4 all jettisoned their bombs; only Nitro 3, Maj. Ted Tolman, continued on to the target. Regarding his MiG kill, Maj. Hunt reported:

"I observed numerous hits and flashes coming from the top of the fuselage just behind the canopy. My piper at this firing position was just forward and a little high on the canopy."

This wartime Air Force photograph is from the collection of James Geer, and depicts 58-1168 starting her engine for another combat mission over North Vietnam. This particular photograph was taken in 1967 while 58-1168 was assigned to the 354th TFS, 355th TFW. On 25 October 1967 this particular Thud was lost to ground fire during an attack on the Paul Doumer Bridge. (USAF / J. Geer Collection)

F-105D / 59-1772
355th TFW / 333rd TFS

Col. Robert R. Scott
Leech 01

355thTFW / 357th TFS

Maj. Harry E. Higgins
Spitfire 01

F-105D-6-RE-59-1772 - During the Vietnam War F-105D 59-1772 claimed two MiG 17s. Col. Scott, Commander of the 255th TFW, downed the first on 26 March 1967 while on a bombing mission in the area of Hoa Loc airfield.

"I concentrated my attention on the nearest MiG 17 and pressed the attack. I followed the MiG, turning inside, and began firing. I observed ordnance impacting on the left wing of the MiG and pieces of material tearing off."

Maj. Higgins claimed the second MiG on 28 April 1967, during an attack on the Han Phong causeway. The following narrative is from Maj. Higgins' MiG claim statement:

"I was approximately 1,500 feet, and I begin to fire the 20-mm cannon. As I prolonged the firing I noticed the MiG begin to smoke, and flames erupted from the left wing root section."

F-105D 59-1772 is seen in this war time photo at Takhli RTAFB, while assigned to the 355th TFW, 333rd TFS, being loaded with 750-pound bombs. This Thud was hit by enemy AAA fire on 20 January 1970 and forced to crash in Laos. (J. Pletcher via D. Hansen)

F-105D / 59-1766
388th TFW / 421st TFS

1st Lt. Karl W. Richter
Ford 03

F-105D-6-RE 59-1766 - Lt. Karl W. Richter was flying as Ford 03 on an Iron Hand mission against a SAM site in the area of the Dap Cau highway and Railroad Bridge when he downed a MiG 17 with 20-mm cannon fire:

"Richter jettisoned his rocket pods, armed his M-61 Gatling gun, and lined up on the left MiG. He made an easy turn as I moved the piper [aiming device] out in front of him and started firing. Richter keeps firing 20-mm rounds at the rate of 100 a minute. Captain Beardsley, his wingman, called, 'You're hitting him! You're hitting him!' Richter saw fire coming out of the back of the MiG."

Do Huy Hoang, the MiG 17 pilot being attack by Lt. Richter, heard a thump:

"The airplane rolled on its own to wings level. Alarmed, he lit the afterburner as the airplane continued rolling right while he tried to regain control. The aircraft responded, but something was wrong." Hoang glanced around and saw that the outer portion of his left wing was in tatters. "I was still flying though, so I just concentrated on staying under control." Richter fired again.

Hoang had just finished checking his engine instruments:

"The VK-1A turbojet was running fine. I thought I was going to be okay, when all of a sudden the plane started to come apart. The instrument panel shattered."

Hoang felt pain in his side and back. He reached between his legs for the ejection handle.

Just as Richter ran out of ammunition, the MiG's right wing broke off. Pieces flew off the tail, and another big chunk flew loose from the MiG. As Richter pulled up to avoid the debris he saw the MiG pilot eject.

This pre-Vietnam Air Force photograph of 59-1766 was taken while she was assigned to the Test, Research, and Development (TRandD) at Nellis Air Force Base in September 1962. Note the 750- or 3,000-pound bombs on the outboard pylons. 59-1766 was lost in combat over SEA on 28 February 1967. (James Geer Collection)

F-105D / 60-424
388th TFW / 13th TFS

Maj. Ralph L. Kuster, Jr.
Hambone 02

F-105D-6-RE 60-424 - While on a strike mission on 3 June '67 against the Bac Giang railroad and highway bridge, Maj. Kuster engaged a MiG 17:

"After being unable to pull lead, and as a last resort, Kuster was able to rotate the F-105 fuselage by rapid aft stick movement enough to put the sight well in front of the MiG. He opened fire at a range of about 200 feet, forcing the MiG to fly through the stream of 20-mm cannon fire. The underside of the MiG's left wing exploded two-thirds of the way between the fuselage and underslung fuel tank."

60-424 is pictured armed in this going to war photograph with six 750-pound bombs and Sidewinder missiles. In the black and white photograph Maj. Kuster has captured the MiG 17 on his gun camera film just seconds before its death. On 10 July 1967, 60-424 was listed as lost in combat after being hit by flak. (P. Martin Collection / USAF)

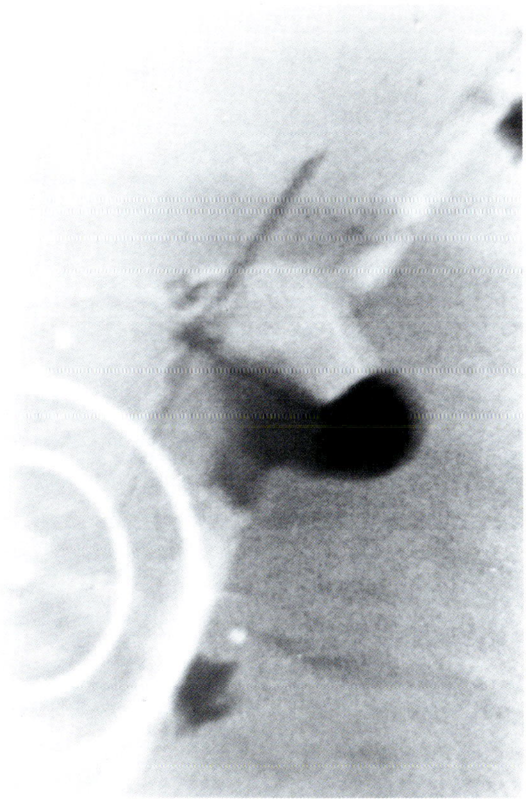

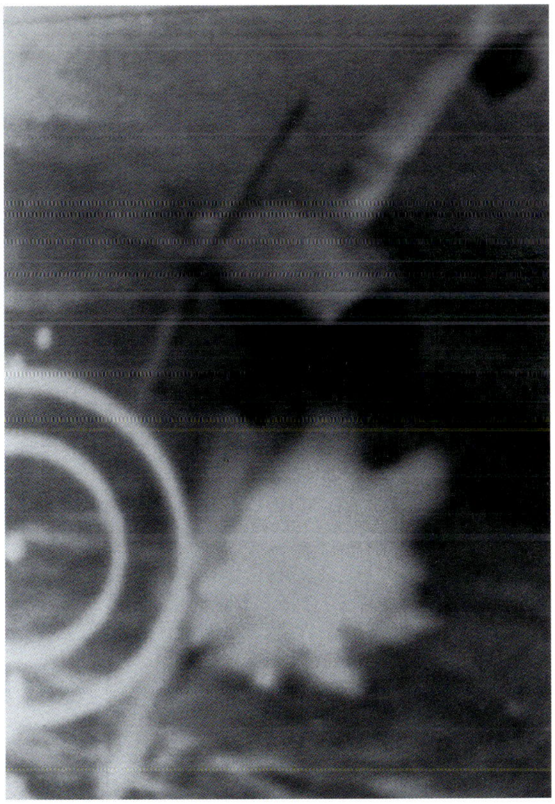

F-105D / 60-458
388th TFW / 34th TFS

Maj. Kenneth T. Blank
Honda 02

F-105D-10-RE 60-458 - While on an Iron Hand mission to destroy a SAM site, Honda flight took two MiG 17s under attack. As a result of the air battle one of the MiGs was destroyed by 20-mm cannon fire from the aircraft of Maj. Blank:

"I fired 200 rounds at a range of 400 to 600 feet before the MiG burst into flames, entered an inverted dive, and hit the ground."

Photographed at Korat, RTAFB, on 29 July 1969, 60-458 is armed with 750-pound bombs and ready for another combat mission into the skies of North Vietnam. (D. Hansen)

F-105D / 60-497
388th TFW / 44th TFS

Maj. Maurice E. Sever, Jr.
Kimona 02

F-105D-10-RE 60-497 - The seventh MiG 17 of 13 May 1967 was downed by Maj. Seaver when he engaged a camouflaged MiG about 1,000 feet away from his position:

"He pulled in behind the MiG and opened fire with his 20-mm cannon. When the MiG was hit, it broke sharply to the right and its wing exploded."

In this photograph obtained from the collection of Pat Martin, 60-497 is taxiing out of the arming pit heading to RP 6. Maj. Seaver's MiG appears in these two black and white photographs from his gun camera film. The second photo clearly shows the MiG exploding. On 18 November 1967 this F-105D was lost in an air battle to a MiG 21.The pilot ejected and was rescued. (P. Martin Collection / J. Seaver)

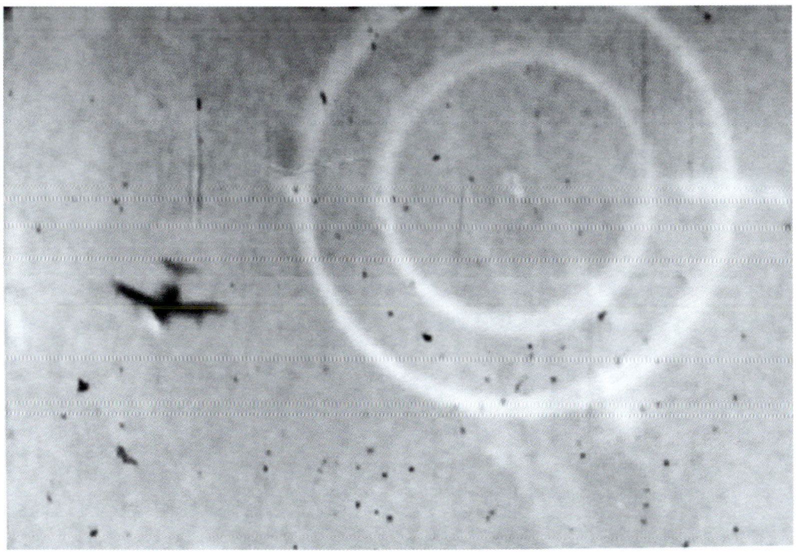

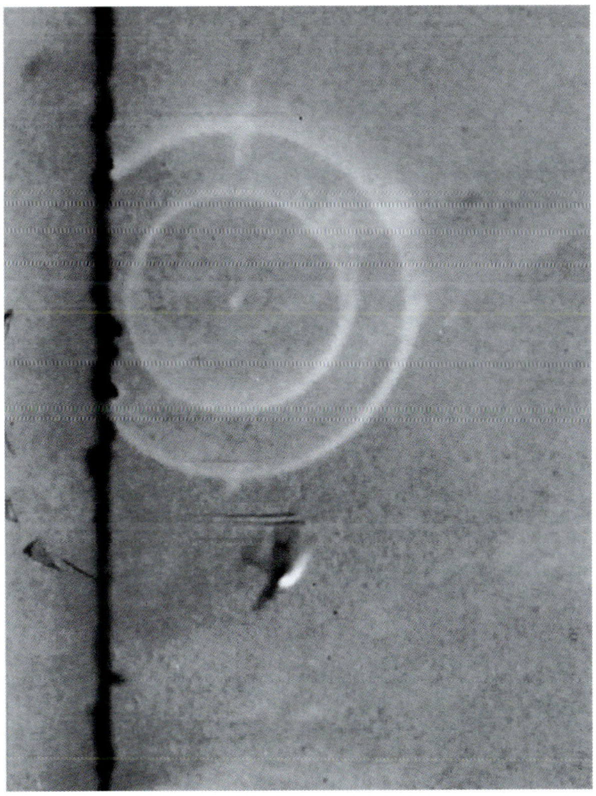

F-105D / 60-498
355th TFW / 44th TFS

Capt. Thomas C. Lesan
Rattler 01

F-105D-10-RE 60-498 - On 30 April 1967, after completing his bomb run on the Northeast Railroad, Rattler lead observed two MiG 17s as he was egressing the target:

"I tracked and opened fire on the number two MiG at approximately 1000 feet. I fired 100 rounds of 20-mm, noting hits impacting down the left side of the forward fuselage and on the left wing. The MiG was last seen with his left wing on fire."

This MiG killer appears in this photograph on a ramp with a second Thunderchief. This photograph may have been taken while she was serving with the Virginia Air National Guard. (P. Martin Collection)

F-105D / 60-501
355th TFW / 354th TFS

Lt. Col. Philip C. Gast
Chevrolet 01

F-105D-10-RE 60-501 - On 13 May 1967 Air Force fighters downed a total of seven North Vietnamese MiGs. Lt. Col. Gast claimed one of the MiGs. Gast stated:

"I began firing my Vulcan gun at 3,000 feet and fired down to minimum range. The MiG never returned fire, and I think I caught him off guard."

On 11 March 1968 this Thud was a non-combat loss in SEA.

F-105D / 60-504
355th TFW / 357th TFS

Lt. Col. Arthur F. Dennis
Atlanta 01

F-105D-10-RE 60-504 - Lt. Col. Dennis was flying lead in Atlanta flight on 28 April 1967. When leaving the target area he spotted a MiG 17 directly ahead of him:

"I closed on the MiG, and when I obtained a missile tone in my head set, I fired the AIM-9. The firing was normal; however, the missile failed to guide. I continued closing to approximately 1,500 feet, began firing, closing to about 700 feet, and the MiG burst into a large ball of fire."

F-105D 60-504 appears in this Paul Minert color photograph when she was assigned to the 357th TFS at Takhli RTAFB. This old Thud was also known as the Memphis Belle II, named after the World War II B-17 bomber. In the second photograph 504 is seen returning from a bombing mission over North Vietnam. This particular F-105 went on to survive the war, and can now been seen at the Air Force Museum in Dayton, Ohio. (P. Minert Collection / USAF)

F-105D / 60-522
355th TFW / 333rd TFS

Maj. Robert G. Rilling
Random 01

F-105D-10-RE 60-522 - During a strike mission on 13 May 1967, Maj. Rilling's flight was part of a large strike package that hit the Yen Vien railroad. While leaving the target area Maj. Rilling encountered enemy MiGs:

"I fired my AIM-9 missile. The missile detonated just to the right and under the tail of the MiG. The aircraft began burning immediately, and pieces were observed falling off the enemy MiG."

F-105D 60-522 is seen in this wartime photograph parked in the revetment area, being readied for a combat mission over North Vietnam, and is seen to be armed with six 750-pound bombs. (T. Helbing)

F-105D / 61-069
388th / 469th TFS

Capt. Larry D. Wiggins
Hambone 03

F-105D-15-RE 61-069 - "A strike mission against the Bac Giang railroad and Highway Bridge, and adjacent railroad yards, produced a confirmed air-to-air victory for Capt. Wiggings, of the 388th. TFW." Wiggins reported:

"The enemy plane attempted to evade the missile but was damaged. The aircraft began trailing a heavy white vapor."

Continuing to close on the MiG as it rolled over and started down, Wiggins fired 376 rounds of 20-mm at a high-angle off. "The MiG exploded in flames and crashed." In this color photograph 61-069 has been completely restored to her wartime markings. As of January 2000, this aircraft has been on display to the public at the SAC Museum in Nebraska. (P. Minert Collection)

F-105D / 61-132
388th TFW / 34th TFS

1st Lt. David B. Waldrop, III
Crossbow 03

F-105D-20-RE 61-0132 - The account of 1st Lt. David B. Waldrop's MiG encounter of 23 August 1967 is reprinted here in its entirety with the kind permission of Lou Drendel and Squadron/Signal Publications:

"The history of aerial combat is filled with examples of great fighter pilots, and most of them could be considered 'naturals.' The gifted warriors are possessed of keen eyesight, the mental acuity to keep track of a complicated tactical situation in their minds as it develops, and a shooting skill which could best compared to skeet or trap shooting.

When Dave Waldrop got his two MiG kills, he had 800 hours total time, with about 450 hours in the F-105. He got the 'long course' at Nellis AFB, Nevada, where he made the acquaintance of Colonel Fritz 'Fox' Treze.

Waldrop's first operational assignment was to Yokota AB, Japan. In may of 1967, the 355th TFW at Takhli RTAFB requested TDY replacements from Yokota. The 355th had lost a lot of experienced pilots, who had finished their tours and were rotated back to the Continental United States. Though they were getting replacements , the new guys were coming straight from RTU and did not have much experience. Waldrop was a bachelor, and knew he would eventually be assigned to one of the combat wings, and he was anxious to go as soon as possible. He volunteered, and when the request for TDY help came he was one of the first Thud drivers sent to SEA from Yokota.

By the following July, he had 45 combat missions, 35 of which were in Route Package Six. The 355th had filled out it's ranks and the TDY help was being sent back to Yokota AB. Waldrop did not want to leave the war zone without finishing his 100 mission tour. Colonel Fritz Treze was then commanding the 44th TFS, of the 388th Wing at Korat RTAFB. Lt. Waldrop called him and applied for a job, which the Fox was happy to give him. Waldrop's narrative of his baptism of fire with the 388th, and MiG killer mission follow:

In wartime the paperwork seems to flow more quickly, and my transfer from the 355th Wing to the 388th literally happened overnight. I flew my first mission with the 388th on 12 August 1967, and it was a big one. We went against the Paul Doumer Bridge in downtown Hanoi. I was number three, and when the flight leader's airplane broke after he dropped off the tanker, he passed lead to me. This was highly unusual. I was just a lieutenant, and lieutenants did not lead anything, but he said; 'hell, you've got 35 missions up here, and that's more than anybody else in the flight so you got the lead!' I got one of the airborne spares, and away we went! I got my flight on and off the target without any problems and returned to Korat.

On the afternoon of 23 August, we were fragged to go against the Yen Vien Railroad Yard, just northeast of Hanoi. It was a big mission, with four strike flights of 105's, two strike flights of F-4s, two F-4 MIGCAP flights, and a Wild Weasel flight. I was Crossbow Three, and was loaded with 750lb. bombs on the centerline, 450 gallon drop tanks on the inboard pylons, an ECM pod on the right outboard pylon, and an AIM-9 Sidewinder AAM on the left outboard pylon. We loaded the element leaders with Sidewinder because we figured they were most likely to get shots at MiGs. Two and four would have pods on both outboard pylons. We flew

in what was called 'pod formations,' which spaced us horizontally and vertically, so as to receive the best electronic countermeasure broadcast coverage from our ECM pods.

We came in from the west, over Laos, and then down the north side of Thud Ridge towards the target, which was only about a mile and a half from Hanoi. As we got closer to the target, 'Big Eye' (the EC-121 radar picket aircraft, which orbit over the Gulf of Tonkin and provide radar coverage of North Vietnam) started calling: 'Bandits, Bandits, Bullseye!' These calls came over guard frequency, and drowned out all radio traffic. Bullseye was Hanoi, and the 'Bandits' call meant that the MiGs were taking off from the airfields around Hanoi. As the MiGs became airborne, we got continuous updates on their position. They were heading west towards us. Their tactics were to swing around behind us and come at us from out of the sun. The MiG 21s would climb to 20,000 feet or higher, get up to mach 1.2 and blow through out formations shooting Atoll AAMs, then zoom back to high altitude before recovering at their home airfields. The 21 was very hard to see, since it is a small airplane to began with, and has a very small frontal area, and leaves no smoke trail when it is in afterburner. Our pod formation was very demanding, since it relied on you to fly a fairly precise profile. You could not 'jink,' and at the same time, you had to keep looking hard for MiGs. Once the MiGs were spotted, and appeared to be after your flight, your only defense was to break into them. The 8th TFW from Ubon RTAFB, with Robin Olds leading, was our MIGCAP on that day, tasked with keeping the MiGs off of the Thud and Phantom strike flights.

As we passed the southern end of Thud Ridge, we turned towards our target. By this time we were getting Bandit calls that indicated the MiGs were turning towards our six o'clock position. Up to that time, we had been doing about 450 knots. As we turned towards the roll-in point, we lit the torch and got up to around 550 knots. Just then, things started to go sour. First, two MiG 21s blew through the F-4s behind my flight, launched two Atolls and knocked down a pair of F-4s. Now there was more noise on guard, as crews of the F-4s called they were hit and then their wingmen hollering for them to bail out, followed by the mournful sound of their beepers going off as their parachutes deployed and they headed for hostile ground.

With all that going on...the adrenaline really...pumping...throat getting dry...head on a swivel looking for more MiGs...I looked forward, through my gunsight, just in time to see the gunsight reticle slide over to the right and die. In spite of everything I tried, I could not bring it back to life. I was heading for the target with no gunsight/bombsight. Oh well, I reasoned, it was a railroad yard (pretty hard to miss), and I had dropped a lot of bombs before and should have a pretty good idea of what the sight picture should look like when I dropped. I pressed on to the target. We had briefed that we would bomb on a heading of southwest, then come off the target hard to the right, heading back to the north for our join-up and egress back up Thud Ridge. There was a lot of MiG 17s in the target area, but they were no factor as I reached the roll-in point. I rolled in and headed down the chute.

As I passed through 7,000 feet, I hit the bomb pickle, then put about six and a half Gs on the airplane as I pulled off the target turning to the north. We tried to never go below 4,000 feet because everybody in North Vietnam had a rifle of some kind, and it was guaranteed they would be shooting. Their effective range was something under 4,000 feet. Six and a half Gs should be enough to ruin any gunners tracking solution, and once I was off the target, I was free to jink as much as I needed to make sure nobody got an easy shot at me.

Pulling off the target, I looked up and saw a 105 in front of me with a pair of MiG 17s 'trapped' at his six o'clock! I never found out who the guy was, but he was in deep trouble. He was straight and level...which you never, never do in the target area, no matter where it is...and he had slowed down to about 400 knots, which made it real easy for the MiGs to stay with him. These two MiGs were right on his ass! Fire was coming out of the left side of the lead MiGs nose as he blasted away at the Thud. His wingman was just sitting back in his wingman position watching what he was sure was a kill for his leader.

This all registered in a split second. I assumed the 105 must be going at least 550, because speed is life in a hostile environment, and you just never, never slowed down up there. Speed was the big advantage the Thud had over everyone else, and I want plenty, so I did something I had never done. I punched off everything...tanks, the MER...they all came off as I put my nose down and lit the afterburner. I called on the radio: 'F-105 heading west, you've got two MiGs on your ass!' This was on my squadron frequency...I hadn't had time to switch to guard, and I guess he wasn't from my squadron, because he never flinched. I planned to dive below the MiGs to avoid being seen, then pulled up and fired my Sidewinder when the MiG was silhouetted against the sky. They were generally headed west, and I was south of them as I accelerated to Mach 1.2, then began to pull in behind them. There was a scattered to broken cloud layer at about 10,000 feet, and I would fire, then zoom past them through the clouds.

As I pulled my nose onto them, my Sidewinder started to growling...it wanted to fly bad! With no gunsight, I knew that using the gun was going to be tough, if not a waste of time, so I figured the Sidewinder was my best bet. But as I looked out front, I saw the Thud, the MiG on his tail, and the MiG wingman. I was ninety-nine percent certain that the Sidewinder was 'seeing' the MiG, but with that big old J-75 engine in the Thud as a possible heat source, I decided not to chance shooting down the 105; I reached up, turned down the volume on the Sidewinder, and decided to use the gun. I was at the MIG's 7 o'clock when I opened up. It doesn't show up on the gun film, but I hit him in the left wing. I saw flashes coming off the left wing. I got off 300 rounds before I realized that I had about 350 knots of overtake. I shot by them, through the overcast, rolled inverted and popped the boards. I was really upset! My one chance in this damn war, and I blew it.

I remained inverted as I looked for a hole in the clouds, hoping to see what had happened. Suddenly, the clouds broke, and there, right under me was a silver MiG 17. He had his afterburner going but was just tooling along by himself, straight and level. I eased my nose down on him, rolled level, and was in a slightly high six o'clock position on the MiG. I opened up on him, and I guess you call this blind-ass luck, because with no gunsight, you wouldn't expect your first rounds to go right through the cockpit, but they did. Some of my luck was training, because we did do a lot of dart shooting at Yokota. I was also fortunate to have flown with Captain Bob Spielman while at Yokota. Bob was a Fighter Weapons School grad and a great air-to-air instructor. That probably accounts for my at least being in the ball park when I started shooting. I fired a total of 250 rounds, which pretty much obliterated the cockpit and chewed up the left side of the fuselage. But the MiG kept flying! A lot of crap had flown off of the MiG, but it didn't burn, blow up, or anything! It just kept flying. I kept clearing my six, expecting the other MiG to start shooting at any time, but there was no one around. I watched as the MiG slowly rolled over and flew into the ground.

My wingman was nowhere around. He had also gotten off on a MiG, and we were separated. I spotted some other Thuds heading out and turned towards them. We were still getting 'Bandit' calls from Big Eye, and it sounded as if they were close to the 105s I was about to join up on! Sure enough, I looked up, and spotted a glint of sunlight high above and behind the Thuds. I turned and started to position myself for a shot at what I realized was a MiG 21. He was just rolling in on the Thuds, when he suddenly leveled his wings, pointed his nose at the high blue and bugged out. Apparently, he had spotted me, or been warned by his GCI controller. I rode all the way out of North Vietnam before I jointed my flight and took on some badly needed gas from a tanker before heading for Korat.

As you might imagine, this flight resulted in a pretty good party at the bar that night. About midway through the party, we got the word that the photo lab had developed the gun camera film, so we all left the bar and went down to Operations. They ran the film, and I really got a surprise. As expected, the film showed the MiG getting nailed, but it also showed something I had not seen during the engagement. An F-105 flew right through the frame while the MiG was getting clobbered, and a big ball of fire blossoms out behind the Thud. (We figured that I gotten his drop tank with a short round) I never saw the guy, and he obviously did not see me. Every 105 drive on that mission was in the room (We all made it back) when that film ran, and not one of them knew who the pilot was that almost got shot down by the MiG, or that flew between me and the MiG I was shooting at. To this day, I don't known who it was.

While all this was going on, we got a call from Robin Olds. He wanted to confirm a kill. I had only claimed one MiG, but based on what Olds said, and the other available information, my wing decided that I had shot down both MiGs. I never saw the first one go down, but Olds did, and he had reason to pay attention—I was told that the MiG would have been his fifth kill, making him the first Ace of the Vietnam War."

This black and white photograph of the Hanoi Special was obtained from Dave Hansen, who is an F-105 historian. 61-0132 sits armed with six 750-pound bombs ready to go to war. F-105D 61-0132 was lost as the result of a mid air collision on 14 May 1968. (D. Hansen)

F-105D / 61-159
355th TFW / 333rd TFS

Capt. Jacques A. Suzanne
Crossbow 01

F-105D-20-RE 61-159 - Capt. Suzanne recounts his MiG engagement of 12 May 1967:

"My flight was trailing Warhawk flight ingressing to the target. At this time a flight of four MiG 17s initiated an attack on Warhawk flight. I turned into the MiGs and tracked two of them. Closing to 4000 feet, I fired one burst of about 200 rounds. The MiGs reversed, and at about 800 feet I fired another burst until minimum range. I observed one MiG pass under my left wing trailing white smoke. The MiG was observed to hit the ground in a bright flash by Crossbow 02."

Parked in revetment B-19 at Takhli RTAFB, 159 and two other F-105s are loaded with six 750-pound bombs. In the second photograph 61-159 is seen ready for take off while serving with the Virginia Air National Guard. The red star of a MiG killer can be seen on the air intake of the left wing. F-105D 61-159 survived the war, and is presently on display at Davis Monthan AFB, Arizona. (T. Brewer via D. Hansen / Flightleader / J. Nixon)

RM
AF
61 159

F-105D / 62-4262
355th TFW / 333rd TFS

Maj. Carl D. Osborne
Random 03

F-105D-30-RE 62-4262 - On 13 May 1967 Maj. Osborne, flying the number three position in Random flight, downed a MiG 17 with a Sidewinder missile:

" I rolled into a slight right bank, and the tone on the AIM-9 peaked up normally. Only a 10-degree left bank was required to hold the reticle on the MiG. The tone was holding well, so I fired the missile, and it began tracking and detonated at the MiG's 3-4 o'clock position.... He immediately turned left and began trailing smoke."

The two black and white photos depict Maj. Osborne taxiing in after his 100 mission over North Vietnam in F-105D 62- 4262. During a mission on 24 October 1967, in the area of Kep airfield, 62-4262 was lost to ground fire. (C. Osborne)

F-105D / 62-4278
388th TFW / 469th TFS

Maj. Roy S. Dickey
Eglin 04

F-105D-31-RE 62-4278 - On only his fourth combat mission into Route Pack VI, Maj. Roy Dickey engaged, fired on, and destroyed a MiG 17 in air-to-air combat:

"As Dickey came off his bomb run he saw a MiG at a 2 o'clock position, attacking Elgin 03. He was then 2,000 feet behind and slightly above the MiG's 4 o'clock position, so he began to fire his 20-mm gun as he closed to within 700 feet. He ceased firing when the MiG burst into flames at the wing root. The entire fuselage behind the cockpit was a sheet of flame."

62-4278 is seen in this color photograph with landing gear down on final approach after a combat mission in the skies of SEA. F-105D 62-4278 was lost over RP 6 to enemy fire. (Aircraft Publicity Burea / M. France)

F-105D / 62-4284
355th TFW / 354th TFS

Capt. Max C. Brestel
Kangaroo 03

Capt. Gene I. Basel
Bison 02

F-105D-31-RE 62-4284 - During her wartime service F-105D 62-4284 was credited with downing three MiG 17s. Capt. Max C. Brestel, on 10 March 1967, claimed two MiGs, and on 27 October 1967 Captain Gene I. Basel claimed the third MiG. Capt. Brestel described the action that led to the destruction of the two MiGs:

MiG 1: "The MiG reversed into a left-hand turn. I fired a two half second burst into him, observing hits in the left wing, fuselage, and canopy. Also observed was a fire in the left wing The aircraft rolled over and hit the ground under my left wing."

MiG 2: "I then closed to within 300 feet of MiG 2, which was firing at Col. Gast. He was in a right turn, and again I fired a two and half-second burst, observing hits in the wing and fuselage. The MiG reversed to the left, and I fired on him again, observing more hits and pieces flying off the aircraft."

On 27 October 1967 Capt. Basel downed a MiG 17 while flying F-105D 62-4284. This engagement took place while his flight was taking heavy and accurate AAA and SAM fire. Capt. Basel reported:

"He didn't see me, and was intent on positioning on an attack on the flight ahead of me until he felt the 20-mm impacts. At the time he reversed his direction abruptly, fire belching from his tailpipe."

Presented here are two outstanding color photographs of 62-4284 from the collections of Don Jay and Ray Leader. The inflight photograph from the Jay collection depicts her with the tail code "RM" and being armed with 6 750-pound bombs. Located on the fuselage are three red stars that denote her three kills. The second post war photograph from the Leader collection depicts 62-4284, while serving with the Oklahoma Air National Guard. Even many years after the war she is sporting the three red stars. (D. Jay / Flightleader)

F-105D / 62-4364
355th TFW / 354th TFS

Capt. William E. Eskew
Panda 01

F-105D-31-RE 62-4364 - During an attack on the Xuan Mai army barracks, Panda flight engaged no less than 11 MiG 17s. The official Air Force records indicate one MiG was downed and three damaged by Panda flight. Though the official Air Force account of the events of 19 April 1967 is accurate in what it represents, it falls far short of the events of that day. The author has interviewed all of the pilots (Captain William Eskew, Capt. Paul Seymour, Capt. Howard Bodenhamer, and Capt. Robert Hammerle) of Panda flight, and the men all claim more MiGs were downed that day than the official Air Force record indicates. Captain Eskew was Panda lead on 19 April 1967 during the two separate air battles that took place that day. There is no doubt in his mind that beside the one MiG that he was officially credited with, other flight members downed MiGs. Captain Eskew told me:

"...regarding MiG kills on 19 April 1967, I'm certain that Howard Bodenhamer and Paul Seymour both scored kills."

Capt. Hammerle is positive that the MiG he engaged that day also went down:

"I know in my heart that was him I saw streaming fire, and I'm sure he had to walk home.:

To quote Captain Eskew:

"The feats and exploits will never be sufficiently recognized, but I known what they accomplished. It was Obviously a MiG Day."

F-105D 62-4364 is seen taking off from Takhli RTAFD armed with 750-pound bombs, looking much as she would have on 19 April 1967 when she flew as Panda lead. 62-4364 was involved in a ground accident in February 1962, and written off as a result of the accident. (USAF / A. Bergeson)

F-105D / 62-4384
Unconfirmed tail number
355th TFW / 354th TFS

Maj. Frederick G. Tolman
Nitro 03

F-105D-31-RE 62-4384 - On 19 April 1967 Maj. Tolman was the only member of Nitro flight to make it to the fragged target (Xuan Mai Army Barracks) and deliver his bombs. While coming off the target Maj. Tolman engaged a MiG 17 that was in pursuit of Nitro lead:

"I closed to gun firing range, at which time the MiG broke hard left. I fired approximately 300 rounds of 20-mm at him and observed hits around his canopy section. The last time I saw the MiG he was trailing white smoke coming from his tail pipe. I saw him roll slowly to the left and start a gentle descent."

F-105D 62-4384 is depicted in this wartime photograph being pre flighted on the ramp at Takhli. The first photograph in this series of photos was taken during May 1967. Pictured in the cockpit is Capt. Al Lenski, and painted on the fuselage to the right of the aircraft's block number "F-105D-31-RE 62-4384" is the red star denoting a MiG kill. There is no official record of this aircraft downing a MiG. However, it is suspect that Maj. Tolman may have flown this jet during his MiG kill mission of 19 April 1967. Air Force records indicate that Maj. Tolman's aircraft sustained minor damage during the MiG kill mission. The record further indicates that 62-4384 sustained battle damage during April 1967 and was in for maintenance to repair that damage. The event that ties Maj. Tolman to this particular F-105D takes place in June 1967. The record is clear that during June 1967, Maj. Tolman flew this jet when he returned fire on the Russian ship Turkestan, which resulted in the death of a number of Russian crewmen. The circumstantial evidence suggests that 62-4384 may in fact be the Thud flown by Maj. Tolman. The final postwar photo depicts this F-105D long after the war on the ramp of the *Virginia*. 62-4384 was lost during March 1981 near Fort Bragg, NC. (R. Wood / A. Lenski via D. Hansen / P. Martin Collection)

RU
384

VIRGINIA
AF 62 384

F-105D / 62-4394
355th TFW / 333rd TFS

Maj. Donald M. Russell
Wildcat 04

F-105D-31-RE 62-4394 - Wildcat flight was part of a strike package fragged to attack the Dai Loi Railroad Bypass Bridge on 18 October 1967. Maj. Russell was flying as Wildcat 03 when he came off the target. During egress he spotted a MiG 17 that passed in front of him, from left to right:

"His left turn helped me get into a good firing position, and I opened fire at an estimated 1000 feet. I noticed flames from both sides of the MiG 17 aft of the cockpit. I followed him for a few moments and saw the fire increase. I lost sight of the MiG as it passed 2000 feet going straight down."

62-4394 is shown in this wartime photograph marked as a double MiG killer. Note the two red stars on the fuselage just under the canopy. There is no record of this jet downing two MiGs during the war. The second head-on photograph shows 62-4394 in the revetment area armed for a morning mission. (P. Martin Collection / USAF via A. Bergeson)

F-105D / UNKNOWN
355th TFW / 333rd TFS

1st Lt. Fred A. Wilson, Jr.
Vegas 02

F-105D- -RE Unknown - During a strike mission on the Dap Cau bridge, Lt. Wilson of the 355th TFW downed a MiG 17 with 20-mm cannon fire:

"The North Vietnamese pilot then suddenly lit his afterburner and pulled up and rolled left behind an F-105."

Flying in the number 2 position in Vegas flight, Lt. Wilson began shooting at the MiG from the 6 o'clock position:

"I just rushed up behind him, firing my 20-mm guns all the time. My sights were not even set up. I just kept firing."

Wilson fired off 280 rounds, shooting off a portion of the MiG's aft section.

F-105D / UNKNOWN
355th TFW / 354th TFS

Capt. Charles W. Couch
Chevrolet 03

F-105D - RE Unknown - On 13 May 1967, Chevrolet flight was tasked to attack the Yen Ven Railroad Yard. After delivering their ordnance on the target they engaged a flight of three MiG 17s:

"We initiated an attack on the MiGs, and as we closed the MiGs must have seen us, because they broke into us. I lined up on their number 2 man and fired a long burst from my 20-mm cannon. The MiG and I were closing head on at this time, and at very close range he broke hard left and disappeared from my view. Another flight in trail with us observed a MiG pilot eject, and a MiG in a spin."

F-105F / 63-8301
355th TFW / 357th TFS

Maj. Leo K. Thorsness
Capt. Harold E. Johnson
Kingfish 01

F-105F-1-RE 63-8301 - On 19 April 1967, Maj. Thorsness and Capt. Johnson were flying the lead aircraft in Kingfisher flight when they attacked an active SAM site. During the egress from the target, and while attempting to locate Kingfish 02, who had been shot down by enemy MiGs, they engaged a MiG 17 in air-to-air combat. The following narrative of that action is taken directly from the original MiG claim statement of Maj. Thorsness:

"The first burst of approximately 300 rounds of 20-mm was fired from an estimated 1500-2000 feet in a right hand shallow pursuit curve, firing with a caged sight reticle. No impacts were observed on the MiG. Within a few seconds we were in the 6:00 o'clock position with approximately 75 to 100 knots overtake speed. I fired another burst of approximately 300 rounds of 20-mm. Pieces began to break off the left wing of the MiG. I pulled up to avoid both the debris and the MiG. While pulling up I rolled slightly to the right, then left. The MiG was approximately 100 feet low and to our left, rolling to the right. The two red stars were clearly discernible, one on top of each wing, and several rips were noted on the battered left wing. We continued in a turn to the left and after turning approximately 130-degrees again sighted the MiG, still in a right descending spiral. Just prior to the MiG impacting the ground Capt. Johnson sighted a MiG 17 at our 6:30 position approximately 2000 feet back. I pulled into a tight left turn, selected afterburner and lower the nose. I again looked at the crippled MiG, saw it impact the ground in what appeared to be a rice field. After confirming the MiG had in fact impacted the ground I made a hard reversal and descended to very near the ground, heading generally westerly into the foothills."

While helping in the RESCAP mission for the downed F-105F, Maj. Thorsness and Capt. Johnson engaged a second MiG 17. Again quoting from Maj. Thorsnees' original MiG claim statement:

"I was able to track the MiG using approximately 30-degrees of bank. I placed the piper ahead and above the MiG and opened

fire at an estimated 2000 feet. Cease fire range was approximately 750-1000 feet. I allowed my piper to slowly slide through the upper wing of the MiG. After approximately two to two and one half seconds of firing the MiG evidently saw our aircraft as he tightened his turn to the left. Just prior to or simultaneous with, the piper sliding through the MiG I observed some large pieces coming off the aircraft. Shortly thereafter I also observed two fuel tanks spraying fuel as they descended."

For his actions on 19 April 1967 Major Leo K. Thorsness was awarded the Medal of Honor. Within days of the 19 April 1967 mission—on his 97th combat mission—Maj. Thorsness and Capt. Johnson were shot down and became POWs for the remainder of the war. True to the motto of the Wild Weasels, "First In Last Out."

Offered here are two excellent wartime photographs of F-105F 63-8301. The second in-flight photo is from the collection of Norm Taylor, depicting 63-8301 armed with Shrike air-to-ground missiles in the skies over North Vietnam. The first color photo is from the collection of Don Logan and shows this historic Thud in the tail code "ZB," armed and ready for another SAM suppression mission. This photograph was taken during the summer of 1968 from a KC-135 tanker. F-105F 63-8301 survived the war, only to be lost on 20 December 1974 in California. (N. Taylor Collection / D. Logan Collection)

F-105F / 63-8317
355th TFW / 357th TFS

Capt. Philip M. Drew
Maj. William H. Wheeler
Otter 03

F-105F-1-RE 63-8317 - On 19 December 1967 Capt. Drew and Maj. Wheeler, flying aircraft 03 in Otter flight, engaged, fired on, and destroyed a MiG 17 in air-to-air combat while on an Iron Hand mission over North Vietnam:

"I had no problem tracking him, so I continued my attack, firing 756 rounds of 20-mm, until I could see the end of the MiG's wing tip on each side of the canopy bow, which put him about 100 feet away. Prior to breaking off my attack I saw numerous 20-mm rounds impacting in his fuselage and right wing root area."

This color photograph of 63-8317 comes from the collection of Pat Martin, and shows the aircraft being readied for another SAM killing mission. This particular Thud was lost in combat in SEA on 30 September 1967. (P. Martin Collection)

F-105F / 63-8329
355th TFW / 333rd TFS

Maj. William M. Dalton
Maj. James M. Graham
Otter 02

F-105D-1-RE 63-8329 - During a SAM suppression mission on 19 December 1967, Majs. Dalton and Graham were credited with half a MiG kill after they finished off a MiG 17 that had been damaged by Lt. George H. McKinney, Jr., and Joseph D. Moore of the 8th TFW. Maj. Dalton offered the following account:

"I closed as much as I could, started tracking, and fired. I fired a short burst, but was not tracking him, so I let up on it, tracked him again, and opened fire. I observed impacts on the left wing and left side of the fuselage under the cockpit, at which time the MiG broke up and left."

F-105D 63-8329 is seen here in the revetment area at Korat RTAFB, ready for combat. This photograph was taken on 20 July 1969 and comes from the David Hansen Collection. (D. Hansen Collection)

Epilogue

By October 1972 the skies over North Vietnam were much as they had been over Nazi Germany in 1945: American warplanes roamed at will, unchallenged and uncontested. The North Vietnamese had virtually no AAA ammunition or SAMs left. They had squandered their principal force of 12 army divisions (leaving only one division in reserve at home) on an invasion that had failed. By every possible measure, North Vietnam in October 1972 had lost the war against the United States.

Why then did the U.S. let up? Why was the Linebacker campaign ended, and bombing North of the 20th parallel brought to a halt? These are questions not for airmen, but for policymakers....

The warriors in the Vietnam War carried out their difficult job with courage and honor. Young men who fought our battles for us did not cause what happened afterward; rather, those events were caused by old men who make policy. Every man who flew against North Vietnam knew from the beginning that the battle could have ended with South Vietnam surviving, not merely for a decent interval, but permanently. It is the diplomat, not the warrior, who must be held accountable if the air war was in vain.

Robert F. Dorr
Air War over Hanoi

Appendix A: North Vietnamese MiGs

The photographs of the MiG 17 and MiG 21 were both taken at the United States Air Force Museum, Wright-Patterson Air Force Base, Dayton, Ohio. Both appear in the colors and markings of the North Vietnamese Air Force. The MiG 19 appears in the colors and makings of the Air Force of Hungary. When and where the photographs were taken is unknown. (Author / W. Hartman)

Mikoyan-Gurevich MiG-17
Fresco

Specifications:
Span: 31 ft. 7 in.
Length: 36 ft. 5 in.
Height: 12 ft. 6 in
Weight: 13,380 lbs. max.
Armament: One 37mm and two 23mm cannons in the lower nose plus 16 rocket in underwing pods, or 1,100 lbs. of bombs
Engine: Klimov VK-1F jet engine of 7,452 lbs. thrust with afterburner
Performance:
Maximum speed: 711 mph.
Cruising speed: 535 mph.
Ranger: 510 miles (1,160 miles with external tanks)
Service Ceiling: 57,000 ft.
Source: USAF Museum

Mikoyan-Gurevich MiG-21
Fishbed

Specification:
Span: 23 ft. 6 in.
Length: 51 ft. 9 in.
Height: 15 ft. 9in.
Weight: 18,080 lbs. max.
Armament: One NR-30 30mm cannon, plus two K-13 A air-to-air missiles
Engine: Tumansky R-11F-300 of 12,675 lbs. thrust (with afterburner)
Performance:
Maximum speed: 1,300 mph.
Cruising speed: 550 mph.
Range: 400 miles
Service Ceiling: 50,000 ft
Source: USAF Museum

Mikoyan-Gurevich MiG-19
Farmer

Specifications
Span: 29.25 ft.
Length: 42.25 ft.
Height: 12 ft. 7in.
Weight: 16,314 lbs.
Armament: Three NR-30 30mm cannons - AA2c 'Atoll' and AA-2d 'Atoll IR'
Engine: Two RD-9B Tumansky Afterbu
Performance:
Maximum Speed: 902 mph with afterburrner turbojets
Cruising Speed: 590 mph
Range: 863 miles
Source: USAF Museum

Appendix B: WANTED

Wanted - anyone who can identify the F-4Cs flown by Captain Lawrence H. Golberg and 1st Lt. Gerald D. Hardgrave of the 8th TFW, 555th TFS, on 30 April 1966, and 1st Lt. Ronald G. Martin and 1st Lt. Richard N. Krieps of the 35th TFW, 480th TFS, on 14 July 1966, during their MiG kill missions.

Wanted - anyone who can positively identify the F-105Ds flown by the following: 1st Lt. Fred A. Wilson, Jr., of the 355th TFW, 333rd TFS, 21 September 1967; Maj. Frederick G. Tolman of the 355th TFW, 354th TFS, 19 April 1967; and Capt. Charles W. Couch of the 355th TFW, 354th TFS, 13 May 1967, during their MiG kill missions.

Can anyone answer the question as to the tail numbers of the MiG killers flown by the 555th Tactical Fighter Squadron during their deployment to Udorn RTAFB from March 1966 to June 1966?

Wanted - anyone who can identify the F-4C depicted in this Frank MacSorley color photograph from the Ron Picciani Collection as a MiG killer. This particular F-4C Phantom was marked as a MiG killer while assigned to the 8th TFW, 555th TFS. It is further known that this F-4C was flown by members of the 555th TFS during their deployment to Udorn RTAFB, March 1966 to June 1966.

If you have any information regarding the questions presented herein, please contact the author at LMAC7041@aol.com, or Thomas Brewer at the Air Force Museum, P.O. Box 1903, Wright-Patterson AFB, Ohio, 45433.

Appendix C: Aircraft and Weapons Combinations Used in MiG Victories

USAF Aircraft	Weapons	MiG-17	MiG-19	MiG-21	Total
F-4C	AIM-7	4	0	10	14
	AIM-9	12	0	10	22
	20-mm Gunfire	3	0	1	4
	Maneuvering	2	0	0	2
	Total	21	0	21	42
F-4D	AIM-4	4	0	1	5
	AIM-7	4	2	20	26
	AIM-9	0	2	3	5
	20-mm Gunifire	4	0	2	6
	Maneuvering	0	0	2	2
	Total	12	4	28	44
F-4E	AIM-7	0	2	8	10
	AIM-9	0	0	4	4
	AIM-9/20mm Gun	0	0	1	1
	20-mm Gunefire	0	1	4	5
	Maneuvering	0	1	0	1
	Total	0	4	17	21
F-4D/F-105F	20-mm Gunfire	1	0	0	1
F-105D	20-mm Gunfire	22	0	0	22
	AIM-9	2	0	0	2
	AIM-9/20-mm Gunfire	1	0	0	1
	Total	25	0	0	25
F-105F	20-mm Gunfire	2	0	0	2
B-52	50Caliber Gunfire	0	0	2	2
	Grand Total	61	8	68	137

Appendix D: USAF Combat Victory Credits Southeast Asia

F-4C

63-7489	14-Jul-66	MiG 21	Swendner/Buttell	35TFW/480TFS
63-7535	5-Nov-66	MiG 21	Latham/Klause	366TFW/480TFS
63-7541	5-Nov-66	MiG 21	Tuck/Rabeni	366TFW/480TFS
63-7577	1-May-67	MiG 17	Dilger/Thies	366TFW/390TFS
63-7589	2-Jan-67	MiG 21	Wetterhahn/Sharp	8TFW/555TFS
63-7623	20-May-67	MiG 17	Pardo/Wayne	8TFW/433TFS
63-7647	5-Jun-67	MiG 17	Pascoe/Wells	8TFW/555TFS
63-7650	16-Sep-66	MiG 17	Jameson/Rose	8TFW/555TFS
63-7652	2-Jan-67	MiG 21	Glynn/Cary	8TFW/433TFS
63-7668	4-May-67	MiG 21	Olds/Lafever	8TFW/555TFS
63-7680	2-Jan-67	MiG 21	Olds/Clifton	8TFW/555TFS
63-7680	13-May-67	MiG 17	Haeffner/Bever	8TFW/433TFS
63-7683	2-Jan-67	MiG 21	Radecker/Murray	8TFW/555TFS
63-7699	14-May-67	MiG 17	Bakke Lambert	366TFW/480TFS
63-7704	14-May-67	MiG 17	Craig/Talley	366TFW/480TFS
63-7710	2-Jan-67	MiG 21	Raspberry/Western	8TFW/555TFS
64-660	12-May-66	MiG 17	Dudley/Kringelis	35TFW/390TFS
64-660	14-May-67	MiG 17	Hargrove/DeMuth	366TFW/480TFS
64-660	5-Jun-67	MiG 17	Priester/Pankhurst	366TFW/480TFS
64-673	20-May-67	MiG 17	Combies/Lafferty	8TFW/433TFS
64-679	10-Jul-65	MiG 17	Roberts/Anderson	2AD/45TFS
64-689	23-Apr-66	MiG 17	Cameron/Evans	8TFW/555TFS
64-693	10-Jul-65	MiG 17	Holcombe/Clark	2AD/45TFS
64-696	29-Apr-66	MiG 17	Dowell/Gossard	8TFW/555TFS
64-697	29-Apr-66	MiG 17	Keith/Bleakley	8TFW/555TFS
64-699	23-Apr-66	MiG 17	Blake/George	8TFW/555TFS
64-720	2-Jan-67	MiG 21	Stone/Dunnegan	8TFW/433TFS
64-739	13-May-67	MiG 17	Kirk/Wayne	8TFW/433TFS
64-748	20-May-67	MiG 21	Janca/Roberts	366TFW/389TFS
64-752	26-Apr-66	MiG 21	Gilmore/Smith	35TFW/480TFS
64-776	23-Apr-67	MiG 21	Anderson/Kjer	366TFW/389TFS
64-776	22-May-67	MiG 21	Titus/Zimer	366TFW/389TFS
64-776	22-May-67	MiG 21	Titus/Zimer	366TFW/389TFS
64-777	20-May-67	MiG 21	Titus/Zimer	366TFW/389TFS
64-797	26-Apr-67	MiG 21	Moore/Sears	366TFW/389TFS
64-829	20-May-67	MiG 17	Olds/Croker	8TFW/433TFS
64-829	20-May-67	MiG 17	Olds/Croker	8TFW/433TFS
64-838	2-Jan-67	MiG 21	Combies/Dutton	8TFW/433TFS

64-839	6-Jan-67	MiG 21	Pascoe/Wells	8TFW/555TFS
64-849	6-Jan-67	MiG 21	Hirsch/Strasswimmer	8TFW/555TFS
		F-4D		
65-608	12-Sep-72	MiG 21	Mahaffey/Shields	388TFW/469TFS
65-784	21-Feb-72	MiG 21	Lodge/Locher	432TRW/555TFS
65-784	8-May-72	MiG 21	Lodge/Locher	432TRW/555TFS
65-784	10-May-72	MiG 21	Lodge/Locher	432TRW/555TFS
65-796	8-Jan-73	MiG 21	Howman/Kullman	432TRW/4TFS
65-801	31-May-72	MiG 21	Ritchie/Pettit	432TRW/555TFS
66-230	30-Mar-72	MiG 21	Olmsted/Volloy	432TRW/13TFS
66-239	9-Sep-72	MiG 21	Tibbett/Hargrove	432TRW/555TFS
66-240	22-Dec-72	MiG 21	Sholders/Binkley	432TRW/555TFS
66-249	5-Jun-67	MiG 17	Raspberry/Gullick	8TFW/555TFS
66-267	9-Sep-72	MiG 19	Madden/DeBellevue	432TRW/555TFS
66-267	9-Sep-72	MiG 19	Madden/DeBellevue	432TRW/555TFS
66-268	12-Oct-72	MiG 21	Madden/Pettit	432TRW/555TFS
66-269	22-Dec-72	MiG 21	Brunson/Pickett	432TRW/555TFS
66-271	18-Jul-72	MiG 21	Baily/Feinstein	432TRW/13TFS
66-271	29-Jul-72	MiG 21	Baily/Feinstein	432TRW/ 13TFS
66-274	26-Oct-67	MiG 17	Logeman/McCoy	8TFW/555TFS
66-280	16-Apr-72	MiG 21	Null/Vahue	432TRW/523TFS
66-7463	1-Mar-72	MiG 21	Kittinger/Hodgdon	432TRW/555TFS
66-7463	16-Apr-72	MiG 21	Olmsted/Maas	432TRW/13TFS
66-7463	8-May-72	MiG 19	Crews/Jones	432TRW/13TFS
66-7463	10-May-72	MiG 21	Ritchie/DeBellevue	432TRW/555TFS
66-7463	28-Aug-72	MiG 21	Ritchie/DeBellevue	432TRW/555TFS
66-7463	15-Oct-72	MiG 21	Ritchie/DeBellevue McCoy/Brown	 432TRW/523TFS
66-7468	28-Dec-72	MiG 21	McKee/Dubler	432TRW/555TFS
66-7501	13-Oct-72	MiG 21	Westphal/Feinstein	432TRW/13TFS
66-7546	26-Oct-67	MiG 17	Gordon/Monsees	8TFW/555TFS
66-7550	16-Apr-72	MiG 21	Cherry/Feinstein	432TRW/13TFS
66-7554	14-Feb-68	MiG 17	Howerton/Voigt	8TFW/555TFS
66-7565	26-Oct-67	MiG 17	Cobb/Lavoy	8TFW/555TFS
66-7594	3-Jan-68	MiG 17	Squier/Muldoon	8TFW/435TFS
66-7601	6-Nov-67	MiG 17	Simmonds/McKinney	8TFW/435TFS
66-7601	6-Nov-67	MiG 17	Simmonds/McKinney	8TFW/435TFS
66-7601	19-Dec-67	MiG 17*	Moore/McKinney	8TFW/435TFS
66-7661	14-Feb-68	MiG 17	Williams/Feighny	8TFW/435TFS
66-7661	11-May-72	MiG 21	Nichols/Bell	432TRW/555TFS
66-7748	3-Jan-68	MiG 17	Bogoslofski/Huskey	8TFW/433TFS
66-7750	24-Oct-67	MiG 21	Kirk/Bongartz	8TFW/433TFS
66-8688	6-Feb-68	MiG 21	Boles/Battista	8TFW/433TFS
66-8690	12-Feb-68	MiG 21	Lang/Moss	8TFW/435TFS
66-8714	5-Feb-68	MiG 21	Hill/Huneke	432TRW/13TFS
66-8719	17-Dec-67	MiG 17	Baker/Ryan	432TRW/13TFS
66-8720	18-Jan-68	MiG 17	Simonet/Smith	8TFW/435TFS
66-8734	10-May-72	MiG 21	Markle/Eaves	432TRW/555TFS
66-8756	12-May-72	MiG 19	Frye/Cooney	432TRW/555TFS
		F-4E		
66-313	6-Oct-72	MiG 19**	Barton/Watson	388TFW/34TFS
67-210	2-Jun-72	MiG 19	Handley/Smallwood	432TRW/58TFS
67-232	15-Oct-72	MiG 21	Rubus/Hendrickson	432TRW/307TFS

67-239	12-Aug-72	MiG 21	Richard/Ettel	432TRW/58TFS
67-268	12-Sep-72	MiG 21	Retterbush/Autrey	388TFW/35TFS
67-270	8-Jul-72	MiG 21	Hardy/Lewinski	366TFW/4TFS
67-275	12-Sep-72	MiG 21	Beckers/Griffin	388TFW/35TFS
67-281	23-May-72	MiG 19	Beckers/Huwe	366TFW35TFS
67-283	21-Jun-72	MiG 21	Christiansen/Harden	388TFW/469TFS
67-292	29-Jul-72	MiG 21	Taft/Imaye	366TFW/4TFS
67-301	15-Oct-72	MiG 21	Holtz/Diehl	388TFW/34TFS
67-333	23-May-72	MiG 21	Beatty/Sumner	366TFW/35TFS
67-362	8-Jul-72	MiG 21	Ritchie/DeBellevue	432TRW/555TFS
67-362	8-Jul-72	MiG 21	Ritchie/DeBellevue	432TRW/555TFS
67-392	2-Sep-72	MiG 19	Lucas/Malloy	388TFW34&35TFSs
67-392	6-Oct-72	MiG 19**	Clouser/Brunson	388TFW/34TFS
68-338	31-May-72	MiG 21	Leonard/Feinstein	432TRW/13TFS
68-338	16-Sep-72	MiG 21	Tibbett/Hargrove	432TRW/555TFS
68-493	5-Oct-72	MiG 21	Coe/Webb	388TFW/34TFS
69-276	8-Oct-72	MiG 21	Retterbush/Jasperson	388TFW/35TFS
69-291	19-Aug-72	MiG 21	White/Bettine	366TFW/4TFS
69-7235	15-Aug-72	MiG 21	Sheffler/Massen	8TFW/336TFS

F-105D

58-1156	29-Jun-66	MiG 17	Tracy	388TFW/421TFS
58-1168	19-Apr-67	MiG 17	Hunt	355TFW/354TFS
59-1772	26-Mar-67	MiG 17	Scott	355TFW/333TFS
59-1772	28-Apr-67	MiG 17	Higgins	355TFW/357TFS
60-424	3-Jun-67	MiG 17	Kuster	388TFW/13TFS
60-497	13-May-67	MiG 17	Seaver	388TFW/44TFS
60-498	30-Apr-67	MiG 17	Lesan	355TFW/333TFS
60-501	13-May-67	MiG 17	Gast	355TFW/354TFS
60-504	28-Apr-67	MiG 17	Dennis	355TFW/357TFS
60-522	13-May-67	MiG 17	Rilling	355TFW/333TFS
61-069	3-Jun-67	MiG 17	Wiggins	388TFW/469TFS
61-132	23-Aug-67	MiG 17	Waldrop	388TFW/34TFS
61-159	12-May-67	MiG 17	Suzanne	355TFW/333TFS
62-4262	13-May-67	MiG 17	Osborne	355TFW/333TFS
62-4278	4-Dec-66	MiG 17	Dickey	388TFW/469TFS
62-4284	10-Mar-67	MiG 17	Brestel	355TFW/354TFS
62-4284	10-Mar-67	MiG 17	Brestel	355TFW/354TFS
62-4284	27-Oct-67	MiG 17	Basel	355TFW/354TFS
62-4364	19-Apr-67	MiG 17	Eskew	355TFW/354TFS
62-4394	18-Oct-67	MiG 17	Russell	355TFW/333TFS

F-105F

63-8301	19-Apr-67	MiG 17	Thorsness/Johnson	355TFW/357TFS
63-8317	19-Dec-67	MiG 17	Drew/Wheeler	355TFW/357TFS
63-8329	19-Dec-67	MiG 17*	Dalton/Graham	355TFW/333TFS

* shared F-4D 66-7601 & F-105F 63-8329

** shared F-4E 66-313 & F-4E 67-392

Confirmed Victories Lacking Serial Numbers

F-4C

	30-Apr-66	MiG 17	Golberg/Hardgrave	8TFW/555TFS
	14-Jul-66	MiG 21	Martin/Kreips	35TFW/480TFS

F-105D

60-458 (?)	18-Aug-66	MiG 17	Blank	388TFW/34TFS
	21-Sep-66	MiG 17	Wilson	355TFW/333TFS
59-1766 (?)	21-Sep-66	MiG 17	Richter	388TFW/421TFS
62-4384 (?)	19-Apr-67	MiG 17	Tolman	355TFW/354TFS
	13-May-67	MiG 17	Couch	355TFW/354TFS

Thomas Brewer
United States Air Force Museum
Dayton, Ohio